Physical Characteristics of the Schnauzer
(from The Kennel Club breed standard)

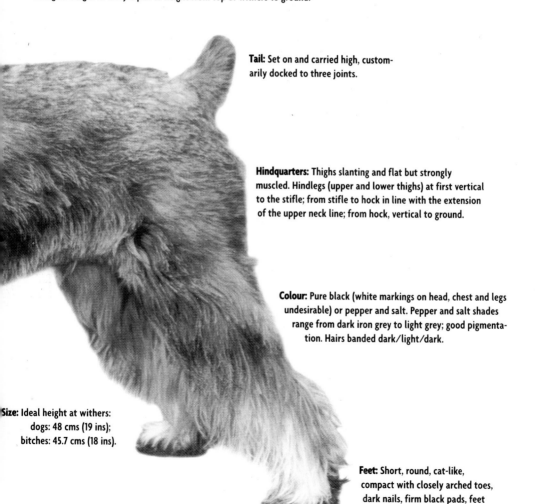

Body: Chest moderately broad; deep with visible, strong breastbone. Back strong and straight. Length of body equal to height from top of withers to ground.

Tail: Set on and carried high, customarily docked to three joints.

Hindquarters: Thighs slanting and flat but strongly muscled. Hindlegs (upper and lower thighs) at first vertical to the stifle; from stifle to hock in line with the extension of the upper neck line; from hock, vertical to ground.

Colour: Pure black (white markings on head, chest and legs undesirable) or pepper and salt. Pepper and salt shades range from dark iron grey to light grey; good pigmentation. Hairs banded dark/light/dark.

Size: Ideal height at withers: dogs: 48 cms (19 ins); bitches: 45.7 cms (18 ins).

Feet: Short, round, cat-like, compact with closely arched toes, dark nails, firm black pads, feet pointing forward.

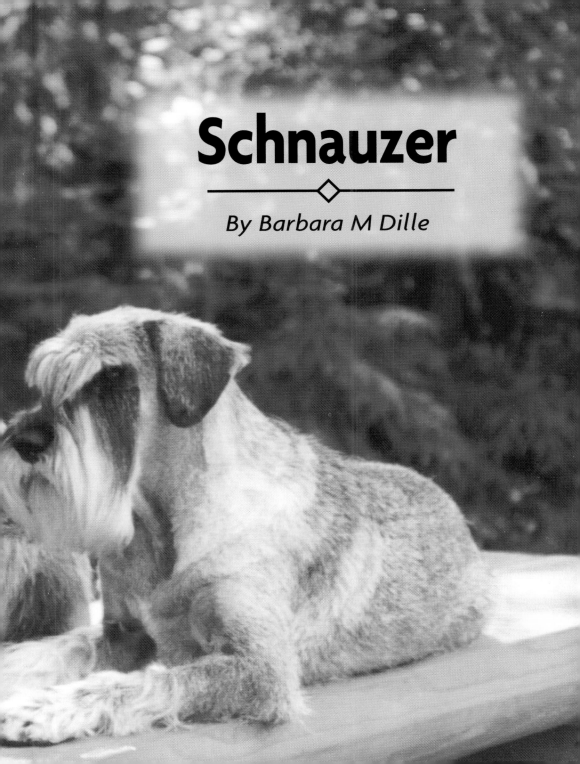

Schnauzer

◇

By Barbara M Dille

Contents

PUBLISHED IN THE UNITED KINGDOM BY:

INTERPET
PUBLISHING

Vincent Lane, Dorking, Surrey RH4 3YX England

ISBN 1-84286-004-6

Photography by Michael Trafford with additional photographs by:

Norvia Behling, TJ Calhoun, Carolina Biological Supply, David Dalton, Doskocil, Isabelle Français, James Hayden-Yoav, James R Hayden, RBP, Carol Ann Johnson, Bill Jonas, Dwight R Kuhn, Dr Dennis Kunkel, Joel Levinson Photography, Mikki Pet Products, Mikron Photography, Niklassou, Phototake, Jean Claude Revy, Dr Andrew Spielman, Tien Tran Photography, Alice van Kempen and Lionel Young Photography.

Illustrations by Patricia Peters.

The publisher wishes to thank all of the owners whose dogs are illustrated in this book, including Clive and Mary Davies, Barbara Dille, L Dobbie, Arden Holst, Carol Karas, Mary Moore, Boel Niklassou, Judy L Rodrick and Mrs Jackie Watson.

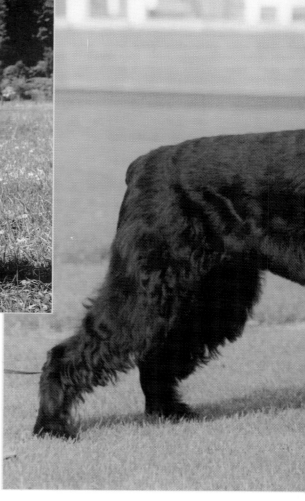

Schnauzers are a celebrated European tradition, dating as far back as the 14th century.

This black Giant Schnauzer is a member of the German Schnauzer breeds. The word *schnauzer* probably derives from the German word *Schnauze*, which means 'snout' or 'muzzle.' The English word *snout* derives from this same German word.

History of the
SCHNAUZER

There is no written record on how and exactly when the Schnauzer was created. Over the years, knowledgeable dog people have discussed many theories. The most frequently heard theory is the one that is probably closest to the truth. This theory relates to tradesmen and farmers in 14th-century Germany who travelled the countryside and markets with carts laden with produce and other wares. The tradesmen needed a medium-sized dog: sizeable and strong enough to be a protection dog for the cart, but small enough to not take up too much space in the cart. These men, being of a practical nature, also desired that this new dog would be of service on the home-front as an excellent ratter, thus capable of double duty by keeping the stable and house vermin-free. The breeders involved most likely crossed the black German Poodle and the grey Wolfspitz with Wirehaired Pinscher stock.

We do know for a fact that the Schnauzer as we know it today appeared in several paintings by Albrecht Durer (1471–1528), the most notable of which was his work entitled *Madonna with Many Animals,* painted in 1492. Durer

Dobermann.

MORE THAN A PINCH OF PINSCHER

The German Schnauzer breeds and the Pinscher breeds were once closely intertwined, so much so that smooth pups (Pinschers) and coarse-haired pups (Schnauzers) appeared in the same litters. In the late 1800s in Germany, the breed(s) were promoted by the German Pinscher-Schnauzer Club.

The standard-sized Pinscher, which is the middle-sized dog between the more popular (and smaller) Miniature Pinscher and the larger Dobermann (known as the Doberman Pinscher in the USA), has never enjoyed the wide acclaim of its Pinscher cousins, though it did figure largely in the history of the Schnauzer. Categorised as a Terrier, the Pinscher remains less common in Germany, though it has been promoted in the UK and USA for the past two decades. In size, it is comparable to the Schnauzer and can be solid red or black and tan (like the Dobermann).

evidently must have owned a Schnauzer, as later works of his contained seemingly the same dog as it aged.

A tapestry entitled *The Crown of Thorns*, dated 1501, by Lucas Cranach the Elder (1472–1553), along with other works of his, also contained the likeness of a Schnauzer. Rembrandt painted some Schnauzers, and one appears in an 18th-century work by the English painter Sir Joshua Reynolds (1723–1792). This makes one wonder if the Schnauzer was in fact in England during the 18th century, or if Reynolds had admired them while travelling on the Continent.

We do know that the Schnauzer, known as the *Mittelschnauzer* in Germany and the Standard Schnauzer in the United States and many other parts of the world, is the origin of the three breeds of Schnauzers,

BRITISH BREED CLUBS

The Kennel Club is the official umbrella club of the pure-bred dog fancy in the UK. In Great Britain, there are two clubs that include the Schnauzer. The Northern Schnauzer Club is for all three sizes, and the Schnauzer Club of Great Britain (SCGB), which was founded in 1929, also includes all three sizes. There are approximately 200 Schnauzer owners in the SCGB.

the Miniature and Giant Schnauzers' being the smaller and larger breeds, respectively. Many people are under the misconception that the Schnauzer is just a larger or smaller version of its more popular cousins, the Miniature and Giant Schnauzers. The truth is that people were so impressed with the attributes of the original (*Mittel* or Standard) Schnauzer that other breeds were introduced into the bloodlines of the Schnauzer to develop the Miniature and Giant Schnauzer breeds that we know today.

Although both the Miniature and the Giant bear a strong physical resemblance to our original Schnauzer, the breeders actually created two distinctly different breeds. The family name Schnauzer that all three breeds share probably derived in the early years of the Schnauzer, due to their distinctive appearance of having hair on their muzzles.

At the third German International show in Hanover in 1879, Wirehaired Pinschers, as they were referred to then, were exhibited for the first time on record. Three dogs were entered from the Wurttenberg kennel, owned by C Berger. The first-place winner was a dog named, fittingly enough, 'Schnauzer.' According to history from then on, all Wirehaired Pinschers were called 'Schnauzers.'

In Germany, where the breed originated, the three sizes of Schnauzer were put into the same club as the Pinschers, and they remain in that club today. In the USA, the Schnauzer, known as the Standard Schnauzer, is exhibited in the Working Group at dog shows along with its larger cousin, the Giant Schnauzer. In the UK, the Schnauzer is shown

COUSINS OF THE SCHNAUZER

The Schnauzer's two cousins differ from him not only in size but also in disposition and temperament. The Miniature, in many cases, is better suited to the less active family with young children. The Giant Schnauzer needs more space and more exercise than the Schnauzer. Like its cousin, the Schnauzer, the Giant is a very strong-willed dog.

Miniature Schnauzer.

EAR CROPPING

Ear cropping consists of surgically trimming the ear leathers and then training the ears to stand upright. Originally, cropping was done to prevent the ears from being bitten by an adversary. With fighting dogs and terriers, cropped ears gave the opponent less to hang on to. Ear cropping also was considered important for cosmetic purposes, as it gives the dog a very smart look.

Fortunately, today the barbaric tradition of cropping ears has been banned in the UK, and dogs with cropped ears cannot be shown. Dogs can be shown in the United States with either cropped or uncropped ears, but they are rarely seen in the ring with uncropped ears.

RIESENSCHNAUZER

The Schnauzer's larger cousin is known in Germany as the *Riesenschnauzer*. This is a very impressive dog with the same colours as the Schnauzer. The Giant's height is 65 to 70 cms (25.5 to 27.5 ins) in dogs, and 60 to 65 cms (23.5 to 25.5 ins) in bitches. Many of the first imports into the UK came from Schnauzer kennels, with the Odivane Kennel of Mary Moore being one of the earliest importers.

From the early 1930s in the UK, these Schnauzers were bred and owned by Capt. L Williams. They are Ch Bodo of Ashways and Bolz v d Brunnenburg of Ashways.

ZWERGSCHNAUZER

The Miniature Schnauzer is known in its country of origin (Germany) as the *Zwergschnauzer*. This smallest of Schnauzers comes in the same colours of solid black and pepper and salt, and additionally silver and black. In some countries, they are also seen in solid white. They stand 33 to 36 cms (13 to 14 ins) at the withers.

made them favourites of both the Red Cross and the German Army.

Although there may have been an occasional Schnauzer imported earlier into the UK, and records show that the first importation of the breed was around the year 1900, the first Schnauzers imported in any great numbers into both the UK and the USA were by the returning World War I soldiers who greatly admired these plucky and courageous dogs. The Schnauzer preceded both the Miniature and Giant into the UK.

in the Utility Group along with its smaller cousin, the Miniature Schnauzer. In fact, until the early 1990s, when the Giant was moved into the Working Group, all three breeds were shown in the Utility Group.

During the First World War, the Germans used the Schnauzer for Red Cross work, and the German Army used the breed for dispatch work. The desirable breed characteristics of medium size, sturdiness and dependability

Nero de Grisons, born in 1943, was an outstanding representative of the breed from the UK. He won numerous awards and produced prize-winning puppies. He was owned by Mrs H H Fergusson.

SCHNAUZER

The Pinscher played a prominent role in the development of the Schnauzer. In the old days, smooth-coated pups were called Pinschers and coarse-haired pups were Schnauzers.

In the USA, the breed quickly gained popularity. In 1925, the Schnauzer Club of America was formed and included fanciers of both Standard and Miniature Schnauzers. In 1933, the club was forced to divide; this division enabled the two sizes to continue to be registered as separate breeds with the American Kennel Club (AKC). The name of the original club was changed to the Standard Schnauzer Club of America (SSCA), with William D Goff as the first president. Since then, several local speciality clubs devoted to the breed have formed around the United States under the auspices of the national club.

In 1934, the AKC presented Mr Goff with a sterling silver cigarette case engraved 1884–1934. One might speculate that this meant that the name for

the Wirehaired Pinscher was officially changed to Schnauzer (*Mittelschnauzer*) in 1884, thus making the breed name 50 years old in 1934.

The Schnauzer has never experienced the same popularity with the general public as the Miniature and Giant Schnauzers. Nevertheless, because of a small group of enthusiastic fanciers, a small amount of growth has been seen. There were approximately 300 pups whelped in the year 2000 in the UK, which accounts for only about 1% of the total dog population. This current lack of popularity has made the task of finding a Schnauzer puppy not always an easy one. Prospective owners have to wait patiently for a pup, especially if the sex of the animal is an important issue.

TWO TOP WINNERS

In the UK, two of the most prominent dogs recently being shown are Ch Siddleys' Barge Master and, the US import from the kennel of Rene Pope, Ch Geistvold Fellow. Both have amassed many Challenge Certificates and both have won multiple Group and Best in Show awards. Keeper of records for all three breeds of Schnauzer dogs, UK judge Brian Braybrook thinks very highly of both dogs and feels that they have been very good advertisements for the breed.

FAMOUS FOUNDATION SCHNAUZERS FROM THE UK

Grauner v Egelsen of Langwood, born in 1926, bred by Fr. Rapp and owned by Capt. C Nash.

Ch Brodick Castle Romper, born in 1936, owned and bred by the Duchess of Montrose.

Ch Craigbourne Lupin, born in 1929, bred by Mrs R G Hornyold and owned by Capt. L Williams.

Ch Salvinia of Dorn Valley, born in 1945, bred by Mrs Laws and owned by Mrs Wallick.

Ch Unity of Langwood.

Ch Blacknest Jolly Good, born in 1950, bred by Mrs Cheshisk and owned by Miss N Witrendge.

Characteristics of the
SCHNAUZER

The Schnauzer is an exciting animal to see and to own. The clean, sharp beauty of this breed is impressive. The lively individualistic personality of the Schnauzer makes him a joy to live with. The Schnauzer is truly one of the most versatile of all breeds. He is small enough for a woman to handle, yet large enough for even the manliest of men. He is robust and sturdy enough to be a working dog, yet small enough in stature so as not to be overwhelming. His ideal size, combined with the breed's properly maintained coat that has minimal shedding and 'doggy odour,' lead many people to think that this is the dog for everyone.

However, nothing could be further from the truth. The breed's combination of intelligence and high spirit can make the Schnauzer more than an handful for a lot of families. This is the dog that many fanciers refer to as 'the dog with the human brain.' Of course, the highly intelligent brain inside this sometimes very quick, active, agile body, when trained properly, does makes the breed a very sensible and reliable working dog...*proper training* being the key.

The mind of the Schnauzer

The appeal of the Schnauzer has led to its considerable fame around the world, celebrated on postage stamps and packaging for various products.

does not develop his full personality as a kennel dog. The Schnauzer's mind develops best with close interactions with his human family. The breed in general has a very clever, inquisitive and sometimes creative bent. These dogs can also have mischievous and sometimes stubbornly determined minds. The Schnauzer has a very strong sense of self-dignity and the dog can be non-forgiving to people and children that have a propensity to tease dogs.

This is a true 'people breed' and the Schnauzer's brain needs the stimulation that only living

DOGS, DOGS, GOOD FOR YOUR HEART!

People usually purchase dogs for companionship, but studies show that dogs can help to improve their owners' health and level of activity, as well as lower a human's risk of coronary heart disease. Without even realising it, when a person puts time into exercising, grooming and feeding a dog, he also puts more time into his own personal health care. Dog owners establish more routine schedules for their dogs to follow, which can have positive effects on a human's health. Dogs also teach us patience, offer unconditional love and provide the joy of having a furry friend to pet!

The abundant facial furnishings are a defining trait of the Schnauzer's appealing look; the facial hair also benefits from daily once-overs, keeping it debris- and tangle-free.

with a family can provide. The Schnauzer is not a one-man dog. Many will pick one family member as their favourite leader, but they readily accept all family members into their inner circle. Children must respect this breed's highly developed sense of self-dignity. They must treat this breed with respect; if they do, they in return will have an extremely loving, loyal chum. Only 'real' family and a few select friends are ever privileged to the 'wiggling from the inside out' tail-wagging welcome the Schnauzer greets his special people upon their arrival home. This is a very selective greeting, one of the distinctive character traits of the breed.

It is not wise to belittle the Schnauzer with needless tricks; he seems to need a reason for everything. Although he does have a good sense of 'dog humour'

HEART HEALTHY

The *Australian Medical Journal* in 1992 found that having pets is heart-healthy. Pet owners had lower blood pressure and lower levels of triglycerides than those who didn't have pets. It has also been found that senior citizens who own pets are more active and less likely to experience depression than those without pets.

at times, in reality he takes his job as guardian of the home very seriously. The family home and car belong to the Schnauzer, and an unannounced visit brings out his deep bark, that from behind the closed door, belies his medium size. He is exceptionally alert to his surroundings and aware of every change in it. His reaction is to hold rather than to attack and, unless provoked, has been known to keep an intruder cornered for quite a long time. Pity is to the letter carrier or delivery boy who does not take the time to make friends with this very big dog in a medium-sized package. His intense attitude at the garden gate inspires respect from all who pass.

The Schnauzer's coat is another feature that sets him apart from most other mid-sized breeds. He possesses a double coat that has an harsh, coarse outer coat consisting of stiff banded hairs that, when seen against the grain, stand slightly up off the back, lying neither smooth nor flat. The undercoat is composed of soft downy-like hairs that should not be so profuse as to overwhelm the topcoat. The undercoat works like insulation, keeping the dog warm in winter and cool in summer. The outer coat offers excellent protection from the elements and easily can be brushed free of dirt.

There are only two acceptable coat colours: the black and the pepper and salt (or salt and pepper). This very distinctive coloration comes about because each of the guard, or outercoat, hairs is actually banded. Depending on the growth state in the hair shaft, it is either black or white. This is where the name for the coat derives: the dog looks like it has been sprinkled with salt and pepper. Texture of both the black and the pepper and salt colours should have the same harsh feeling.

The ears in the UK and many parts of the Continent must be kept in their natural state, as ear cropping is forbidden by law. Even the tail in some countries on the Continent must remain undocked, due to new laws against tail docking. In the UK, if a breeder wants tails docked, a licensed veterinary surgeon must do them. In the US, where no law prohibits either ear cropping or tail docking, the cropped ears and docked tails are the norm with

DO YOU WANT TO LIVE LONGER?

If you like to volunteer, it is wonderful if you can take your dog to a nursing home once a week for several hours. The elder community loves to have a dog with which to visit, and often your dog will bring a bit of companionship to someone who is lonely or somewhat detached from the world. You will be not only bringing happiness to someone else but also keeping your dog busy—and we haven't even mentioned the fact that it has been discovered that volunteering helps to increase your own longevity!

Schnauzers on the Continent today can be seen with undocked tails and natural drop ears.

The American version of the Schnauzer has cropped ears and a docked tail.

most breeders, as they feel it makes for a sharper, crisper, more attention-getting dog.

With the quarantine now lifted, with dogs being able to come into the UK with a 'pet passport,' it will be interesting to see how the breed fares and how it will look in the future. I imagine that the tradesmen that originally drew up the blueprint for this breed would find it hard for the current trend of Schnauzers to survive in their carts and in the stable yards of yester-year. Back then, the ears were cropped so the rats could not get them, and the tails were docked so they would not get caught in the wagon wheels.

SCHNAUZER

A Schnauzer (as well as every other dog) competing in a dog show is measured against its breed standard. The Schnauzer that is closest to the ideal dog described in the standard is declared the winner.

Breed Standard for the
SCHNAUZER

Considered the 'yardstick' by which the Schnauzer is assessed by breeders and judges in Britain, The Kennel Club standard for the Schnauzer describes what is, indeed, the ideal representative of the breed. It is the standard to which dogs competing in dog shows are compared. The dog that most closely conforms to the standard, in the judge's opinion, is declared the winner (class winner, Best of Breed, etc). Breeders rely on the show ring as the proving ground of their programmes. Only Schnauzers who have been recognised in the show ring are thereby worthy of including in a breeder's programme.

There are many different standards for the Schnauzer throughout the world, each kennel club adopting a different, though vastly similar, standard for the breed. The American Kennel Club (AKC) uses its own standard, and the Fédération Cynologique Internationale (FCI) uses its own (which is, in fact, the German standard, from the Schnauzer's native country). If you are planning on exhibiting your Schnauzer outside the UK, you must be aware of the differ-

ences between the standards from country to country. These will vary beyond ear cropping and tail docking to finer points of conformation.

It is wise to attend breeder

BREEDER'S BLUEPRINT

If you are considering breeding your bitch, it is very important that you are familiar with the breed standard. Reputable breeders breed with the intention of producing dogs that are as close as possible to the standard and that contribute to the advancement of the breed. Study the standard for both physical appearance and temperament, and make certain your bitch and your chosen stud dog measure up.

Correct type and conformation for the head.

seminars and a few dog shows to help you better understand The Kennel Club standard. Reading a standard is largely based on personal interpretation, as the standard is a somewhat vague guide to a very specific animal. Words like 'medium,' 'strong' and 'high' are relatively meaningless without being able to see actual quality specimens (so you can appreciate just how medium, strong and high a particular feature should be).

The standard bears reading and re-reading, as often even experienced breeders need to be reminded of every aspect of the description provided herein. Discuss the standard with breeders and exhibitors at shows. This is a good way to make the standard come alive for you.

THE KENNEL CLUB STANDARD FOR THE SCHNAUZER

General Appearance: Sturdily built, robust, sinewy, nearly square (length of body equal to height at shoulders). Expression keen and attitude alert. Correct conformation is of more importance than colour or purely 'beauty' points.

Characteristics: Strong, vigorous dog capable of great endurance.

Temperament: Alert, reliable and intelligent. Primarily a companion dog.

Head and Skull: Head strong and of good length, narrowing from ears to eyes and then gradually forward toward end of nose. Upper part of the head (occiput to the base of the forehead) moderately broad between ears. Flat, creaseless forehead; well muscled but not too strongly developed cheeks. Medium stop to accentuate prominent eyebrows. Powerful muzzle ending in a moderately blunt line, with bristly, stubby moustache and chin whiskers. Ridge of nose straight and running almost parallel to extension of forehead. Nose black with wide nostrils. Lips tight but not overlapping.

Eyes: Medium-sized, dark, oval, set forward with arched bushy eyebrows.

Ears: Neat, V-shaped, set high and dropping forward to temple.

Mouth: Jaws strong, with a perfect, regular and complete scissor bite, i.e. upper teeth closely overlapping lower teeth and set square to the jaws.

Neck: Moderately long, strong, and slightly arched; skin close to throat; neck set cleanly on shoulders.

Forequarters: Shoulders flat and well laid. Forelegs straight viewed from any angle. Muscles smooth and lithe rather than prominent; bone strong, straight and carried well down to feet; elbows close to body and pointing directly backward.

Body: Chest moderately broad; deep with visible, strong breast-bone reaching at least to height of elbow and rising slightly backward to loins. Back strong and straight, slightly higher at shoulder than at hindquarters, with short, well developed loins.

FOUR EXAMPLES OF FAULTY BODIES

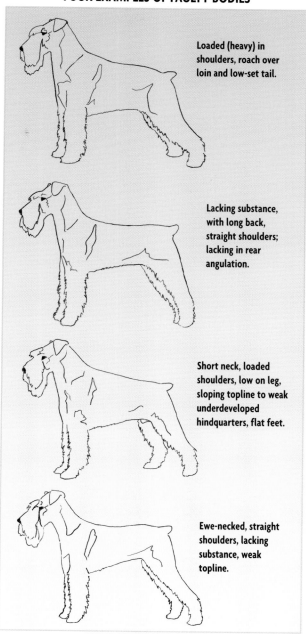

Loaded (heavy) in shoulders, roach over loin and low-set tail.

Lacking substance, with long back, straight shoulders; lacking in rear angulation.

Short neck, loaded shoulders, low on leg, sloping topline to weak underdeveloped hindquarters, flat feet.

Ewe-necked, straight shoulders, lacking substance, weak topline.

Ribs well sprung. Length of body equal to height from top of withers to ground.

Hindquarters: Thighs slanting and flat but strongly muscled. Hindlegs (upper and lower thighs) at first vertical to the stifle; from stifle to hock in line with the extension of the upper neck line; from hock, vertical to ground.

Feet: Short, round, cat-like, compact with closely arched toes, dark nails, firm black pads, feet pointing forward.

Tail: Set on and carried high, customarily docked to three joints.

Gait/Movement: Free, balanced and vigorous, with good reach in forequarters and good driving power in hindquarters. Topline remains level in action.

Coat: Harsh, wiry and short enough for smartness. Closer on neck and shoulders; clean on throat, skull and ears. Harsh hair on legs. Dense undercoat essential.

Colour: Pure black (white markings on head, chest and legs undesirable) or pepper and salt. Pepper and salt shades range from dark iron grey to light grey; good pigmentation. Hairs banded dark/light/dark. Facial mask to harmonise with corresponding coat colour.

Size: Ideal height at withers: dogs: 48 cms (19 ins); bitches: 45.7 cms (18 ins). Any variations of more than 2.5 cms (1 in) in these heights undesirable.

Faults: Any departure from the foregoing points should be considered a fault and the seriousness with which the fault should be regarded should be in exact proportion to its degree.

Note: Male animals should have two apparently normal testicles fully descended into the scrotum.

THINK BEFORE YOU BREED
The decision to breed your dog is one that must be considered carefully and researched thoroughly before moving into action. Some people believe that breeding will make their bitches happier or that it is an easy way to make money. Unfortunately, indiscriminate breeding only worsens the rampant problem of pet overpopulation, as well as putting a considerable dent in your pocketbook. As for the bitch, the entire process from mating through whelping is not an easy one and puts your pet under considerable stress. Last, but not least, consider whether or not you have the means to care for an entire litter of pups. Without a reputation in the field, your attempts to sell the pups may be unsuccessful.

Comparison of the three schnauzer breeds, based on ideal heights for males: Miniature Schnauzer, (Standard) Schnauzer and Giant Schnauzer.

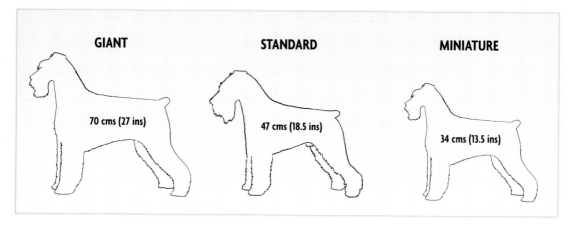

GIANT

70 cms (27 ins)

STANDARD

47 cms (18.5 ins)

MINIATURE

34 cms (13.5 ins)

PUPPY APPEARANCE

Your puppy should have a well-fed appearance but not a distended abdomen, which may indicate worms or incorrect feeding, or both. The body should be firm, with a solid feel. The skin of the abdomen should be pale pink and clean, without signs of scratching or rash. Check the hind legs to make certain that dewclaws were removed, if any were present at birth.

WHERE TO BEGIN?

If you are convinced that the Schnauzer is the ideal dog for you, it's time to learn about where to find a puppy and what to look for. The puppy selection process is not one that should be rushed, so be patient and do all your homework. You should enquire about established breeders who enjoy a good reputation in the breed. You are looking for a breeder with experience in dogs, outstanding dog ethics and a strong commitment to the breed.

New owners should have as many questions as they have doubts. An experienced Schnauzer breeder is indeed the one to answer your many questions and make you comfortable with your choice of the Schnauzer. An established breeder will sell you a puppy at a fair price if, and only if, the breeder determines that you are a suitable, worthy owner of his dogs. An established breeder can be relied upon for advice, no matter what time of day or night. A reputable breeder will accept a puppy back, without questions, should you decide that this is not the right dog for you.

When a prospective owner goes looking for a pup, I suggest interviewing several breeders by telephone. You must be able to relate to the breeder personally, as you will most likely be in contact with him often in the first year or two after bringing your pup home.

When choosing a breeder, reputation is much more important than convenience of location. If you have to drive to the opposite side of the island to purchase the best puppy, then so be it...fill up the tank with petrol and carry on! The Kennel Club is able to recommend breeders of quality Schnauzers, as can any local all-breed club or Schnauzer club.

Potential owners are encouraged to attend dog shows (or trials) to see the Schnauzers in action, to meet the owners and handlers firsthand and to get an idea of what Schnauzers look like outside a photographer's lens. Provided you approach the handlers when they are not terribly busy with the dogs, most are more than willing to answer questions, recommend breeders and give advice.

Once you have contacted and met a breeder or two and made your choice about which breeder is best suited to your needs, it's time to visit the litter. Considering how relatively uncommon the Schnauzer is in most countries, most top breeders will have

PREPARING FOR PUP

Unfortunately, when a puppy is bought by someone who does not take into consideration the time and attention that dog ownership requires, it is the puppy who suffers when he is either abandoned or placed in a shelter by a frustrated owner. So all of the 'homework' you do in preparation for your pup's arrival will benefit you both. The more informed you are, the more you will know what to expect and the better equipped you will be to handle the ups and downs of raising a puppy. Hopefully, everyone in the household is willing to do his part in raising and caring for the pup. The anticipation of owning a dog often brings a lot of promises from excited family members: 'I will walk him every day,' 'I will feed him,' 'I will house-train him,' etc., but these things take time and effort, and promises can easily be forgotten once the novelty of the new pet has worn off.

waiting lists. Sometimes new owners have to wait as long as two years for a puppy. If you are really committed to the breeder whom you've selected, then you will wait (and hope for an early arrival!).

You must be familiar with the breed standard when looking at the dam of the puppies and at the puppies themselves. If the dam is a champion, your chances of getting a well-made puppy is increased. Try to pick a pup with the personality that you like, and with conformation closest to the standard. Of course, the puppy should be healthy and look in good condition. Make absolutely sure to take the breed standard with you when looking for a pup. A reputable breeder will appreciate that you have done your homework in learning more about our wonderful breed.

Picking a puppy is very difficult, even for the seasoned

DID YOU KNOW?
You should not even think about buying a puppy that looks sick, undernourished, overly frightened or nervous. Sometimes a timid puppy will warm up to you after a 30-minute 'let's-get-acquainted' session.

owner. I feel that usually the breeder, who observes the litter several times a day for the first weeks of the pups' lives, knows best which puppy will grow up to be the best dog for you and your family. This especially holds true for the breeder with many years of experience. Since Schnauzers generally have large litters, averaging six to ten puppies, selection should be exciting once a desirable litter becomes available.

Always check the bite of your selected puppy to be sure that it is neither overshot nor undershot. This may not be too noticeable on a young puppy, but will become more evident as the puppy gets older. Sometimes a bite that is slightly 'off' will fix itself, while other times it will worsen. Discuss this with your breeder if you are concerned. Even if you are not going to show the dog, it is only naturally preferable to acquire a Schnauzer who does not have a noticeable defect (which could affect the dog's eating as well).

Breeders commonly allow visitors to see their litters by around the fifth or sixth week, and puppies leave for their new homes between the eighth and tenth week. Breeders who permit their puppies to leave early are more interested in your pounds than in their puppies' well-being. Puppies need to learn the rules of the pack from their dams, and most dams continue teaching the pups manners and dos and don'ts until around the eighth week. Breeders spend significant amounts of time with the Schnauzer toddlers so that the pups are able to interact with the 'other species,' i.e. humans. Given the long history that dogs and humans have, bonding between the two species is natural but must be nurtured. A well-bred, well-socialised Schnauzer pup wants nothing more than to be near you and please you.

COMMITMENT OF OWNERSHIP

After considering all of these factors, you have most likely already made some very important decisions about selecting your puppy. You have chosen a Schnauzer, which means that you have decided which characteristics you want in a dog and which type of dog will best fit into your family and lifestyle. If you have selected a breeder, you have gone a step further—you have done your research and

PUPPY SELECTION

Your selection of a good puppy can be determined by your needs. A show potential or a good pet? It is your choice. Every puppy, however, should be of good temperament. Although show-quality puppies are bred and raised with emphasis on physical conformation, responsible breeders strive for equally good temperament. Do not buy from a breeder who concentrates solely on physical beauty at the expense of personality.

DOCUMENTATION

Two important documents you will get from the breeder are the pup's pedigree and registration certificate. The breeder should register the litter and each pup with The Kennel Club, and it is necessary for you to have the paperwork if you plan on showing or breeding in the future.

Make sure you know the breeder's intentions on which type of registration he will obtain for the pup. There are limited registrations which may prohibit the dog from being shown, bred or competing in non-conformation trials such as Working or Agility if the breeder feels that the pup is not of sufficient quality to do so. There is also a type of registration that will permit the dog in non-conformation competition only.

On the reverse side of the registration certificate, the new owner can find the transfer section, which must be signed by the breeder.

Puppies may look like decorative objects, but they are living, breathing, demanding creatures. Make your decision to own a Schnauzer with care and responsibility. Don't be whimsical...you are choosing a family member.

found a responsible, conscientious person who breeds quality Schnauzers and who should be a reliable source of help as you and your puppy adjust to life together. If you have observed a litter in action, you have obtained a firsthand look at the dynamics of a puppy 'pack' and, thus, you have learned about each pup's individual personality—perhaps you have even found one that particularly appeals to you.

However, even if you have not yet found the Schnauzer puppy of your dreams, observing pups will help you learn to recognise certain behaviour and to determine what a pup's behaviour indicates about his temperament. You will be able to pick out which pups are the leaders, which ones are less outgoing, which ones are confident, which ones are shy, playful, friendly, aggressive, etc. Equally as important, you will learn to recognise what an healthy pup should look and act like. All of these things will help you in your search, and when you find the Schnauzer that was meant for you, you will know it!

Researching your breed, selecting a responsible breeder and observing as many pups as possible are all important steps on the way to dog ownership. It may seem like a lot of effort…and you have not even taken the pup home yet! Remember, though, you cannot be too careful when it comes to deciding on the type of dog you want and finding out about your prospective pup's background. Buying a puppy is not—or should not be—just another whimsical purchase. This is one instance in which you actually do get to choose your own family! You may be thinking that buying a puppy should be fun—it should not be so serious and so much work. Keep in mind that your puppy is not a cuddly stuffed toy or decorative lawn ornament; rather, he is a living creature that will become a real member of your family. You will come to realise that, while buying

DOG OR BITCH?

Male Schnauzers can be dog-aggressive. Most males will not deliberately start a fight, but they are always willing to finish it. A sexually active male is more prone to defend whatever he imagines as his territory. If there are no females living with them, two or more males can be raised together. If you plan to have two or more males living together, neutering all of them is highly recommended unless they are being shown or used as breeding stock.

Females on the whole are not dog-aggressive to their own kind, except during the first few weeks of raising puppies. Some females will 'not so politely' tell a strange male to keep his distance. When males and females are housed together, in many cases the female is the dominant leader of the dog pack.

INSURANCE

Many good breeders will offer you insurance with your new puppy, which is an excellent idea. The first few weeks of insurance will probably be covered free of charge or with only minimal cost, allowing you to take up the policy when this expires. If you own a pet dog, it is sensible to take out such a policy as veterinary fees can be high, although routine vaccinations and boosters are not covered. Look carefully at the many options open to you before deciding which suits you best.

a puppy is a pleasurable and exciting endeavour, it is not something to be taken lightly. Relax…the fun will start when the pup comes home!

Always keep in mind that a puppy is nothing more than a baby in a furry disguise…a baby who is virtually helpless in a

THE FAIRER SEX

An important consideration to be discussed is the sex of your puppy. For a family companion, a bitch may be the better choice, considering the female's inbred concern for all young creatures and her accompanying tolerance and patience. It is always advisable to spay a pet bitch, which may guarantee her a longer life.

YOUR SCHEDULE . . .

If you lead an erratic, unpredictable life, with daily or weekly changes in your work requirements, consider the problems of owning a puppy. The new puppy has to be fed regularly, socialised (loved, petted, handled, introduced to other people) and, most importantly, allowed to visit outdoors for toilet training. As the dog gets older, it can be more tolerant of deviations in its feeding and toilet relief.

human world and who trusts his owner for fulfilment of his basic needs for survival. In addition to food, water and shelter, your pup needs care, protection, guidance and love. If you are not prepared to commit to this, then you are not prepared to own a dog.

Wait a minute, you say. How hard could this be? All of my neighbours own dogs and they seem to be doing just fine. Why should I have to worry about all of this? Well, you should not worry about it; in fact, you will probably find that once your Schnauzer pup gets used to his new home, he will fall into his place in the family quite naturally. However, it never hurts to emphasise the commitment of dog ownership. With some time and patience, it is really not too difficult to raise a curious and exuberant Schnauzer pup to be a well-adjusted and well-mannered adult dog—a dog that could be your most loyal friend.

HOME PREPARATION FOR THE PUP

Researching your breed and finding a breeder are only two aspects of the 'homework' you will have to do before taking your Schnauzer puppy home. You will also have to prepare your home and family for the new addition. Much as you would prepare a nursery for a newborn baby, you will need to designate a place in your home that will be the puppy's own. How you prepare your home will depend on how much freedom the dog will be allowed. Whatever you decide, you must ensure that he has a place that he can 'call his own.'

When you bring your new puppy into your home, you are bringing him into what will become his home as well. Obviously, you did not buy a puppy with the intentions of catering to his every whim and allowing him to 'rule the roost,'

DID YOU KNOW?

Breeders rarely release puppies until they are eight to ten weeks of age. This is an acceptable age for most breeds of dog, excepting toy breeds, which are not released until around 12 weeks, given their petite sizes. If a breeder has a puppy that is 12 weeks of age or older, it is likely well socialised and house-trained. Be sure that it is otherwise healthy before deciding to take it home.

but in order for a puppy to grow into a stable, well-adjusted dog, he has to feel comfortable in his surroundings. Remember, he is leaving the warmth and security of his mother and littermates, as well as the familiarity of the only place he has ever known, so it is important to make his transition as easy as possible. By preparing a place in your home for the puppy, you are making him feel as welcome as possible in a strange new place. It should not take him long to get used to it, but the sudden shock of being transplanted is somewhat traumatic for a young pup. Imagine how a small child would feel in the same situation—that is how your puppy must be feeling. It is up to you to reassure him and to let him know, 'Little chap, you are going to like it here!'

Include the children when selecting your Schnauzer puppy. Puppies often automatically take to young children and form a lasting bond.

PHOTO COURTESY OF DOSKOCIL

WHAT YOU SHOULD BUY

CRATE

To someone unfamiliar with the use of crates in dog training, it may seem like punishment to shut a dog in a crate, but this is not the case at all. Although all breeders do not advocate crate training, more and more breeders and trainers are recommending crates as preferred tools for show puppies as well as pet puppies. Crates are not cruel—crates have many humane and highly effective uses in dog care and training. For example, crate training is a very popular and very successful house-training method. In addition, a crate can keep your dog safe during travel and, perhaps most importantly, a crate provides your dog with a place of his own in your home. It serves as a 'doggie bedroom' of sorts—your Schnauzer can curl up in his crate when he wants to sleep or when he just needs a break. Many dogs sleep in their crates overnight. With soft bedding and his favourite toy, a crate becomes a cosy pseudo-den for your dog. Like his ancestors, he too will seek out the comfort and retreat of a den—you just happen to be providing him with something a little more luxurious than what his early ancestors enjoyed.

As far as purchasing a crate, the type that you buy is up to you. It will most likely be one of the two most popular types: wire or fibreglass. There are advantages and disadvantages to each type. For example, a wire crate is more open, allowing the air to flow through and affording the dog a view of what is going on around him, while a fibreglass crate is sturdier. Both can double as travel crates, providing protection for the dog.

The size of the crate is another

thing to consider. Most adult Schnauzers can very comfortably sleep in a medium-sized crate, approximately 76 cms (30 inches) long by 53 cms (21 inches) wide by 61 cms (24 inches) high. A smaller area is recommended when using a crate for house-training purposes. By using the crate method for toilet training, a Schnauzer pup can be taught to keep the kennel and house clean relatively quickly, compared to some other breeds.

BEDDING

Veterinary bedding in the dog's crate will help the dog feel more at home, and you may also like to pop in a small blanket. First, this will take the place of the leaves, twigs, etc., that the pup would use in the wild to make a den; the pup can make his own 'burrow' in the crate. Although your pup is far removed from his den-making ancestors, the denning instinct is still a part of his genetic makeup. Second, until you take your pup home, he has been sleeping amid the warmth of his mother and littermates, and while a blanket is not the same as a warm, breathing body, it still provides heat and something with which to snuggle. You will want to wash your pup's bedding frequently in case he has a toileting 'accident' in his crate, and replace or remove any blanket that becomes ragged and starts to fall apart.

CRATE TRAINING TIPS

During crate training, you should partition off the section of the crate in which the pup stays. If he is given too big an area, this will hinder your training efforts. Crate training is based on the fact that a dog does not like to soil his sleeping quarters, so it is ineffective to keep a pup in a crate that is so big that he can eliminate in one end and get far enough away from it to sleep. Also, you want to make the crate den-like for the dog. Blankets and a favourite toy will make the crate cosy for the small pup; as he grows, you may want to evict some of his 'roommates' to make more room.

It will take some coaxing at first, but be patient. Given some time to get used to it, your Schnauzer will adapt to his new home-within-a-home quite nicely.

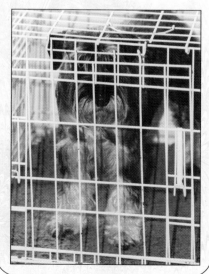

Toys

Toys are a must for dogs of all ages, especially for curious playful pups. Puppies are the 'children' of the dog world, and what child does not love toys?

> **PLAY'S THE THING**
>
> Teaching the dog to play with his toys in running and fetching games is an ideal way to help the dog develop muscle, learn motor skills and bond with you, his owner and master.
>
> He also needs to learn how to inhibit his bite reflex and never to use his teeth on people, forbidden objects and other animals in play. Whenever you play with your dog, you make the rules. This becomes an important message to your dog in teaching him that you are the pack leader and control everything he does in life. Once your dog accepts you as his leader, your relationship with him will be cemented for life.

Chew toys provide enjoyment for both dog and owner—your dog will enjoy playing with his favourite toys, while you will enjoy the fact that they distract him from chewing on your expensive shoes and leather sofa. Puppies love to chew; in fact, chewing is a physical need for pups as they are teething, and everything looks appetising! The full range of your possessions—from old tea towel to Oriental carpet—are fair game in the eyes of a teething pup. Puppies are not all that discerning when it comes to finding something literally to 'sink their teeth into'—everything tastes great!

Most Schnauzers are chewers, not only during puppyhood but also throughout their adult lives. Luckily, they can be taught to chew only on appropriate dog toys. The Schnauzer is a very intelligent dog and consequently gets bored easily. Try using a toy box or basket filled with many different shapes, textures and sizes of toys. Stuffed plush animals are very much favoured, and most Schnauzers delight in 'de-stuffing' them, but will continue to play with them even after the stuffing is all gone. These unstuffed wet plush carcasses are usually the ones picked up by Schnauzers when greeting guests at the door. Be careful that the dog doesn't eat the 'innards' of these toys, as this can be dangerous.

Soft natural latex squeak toys are also favourites, but these too must be carefully monitored that they are not torn apart and the squeakers eaten. Hard toys such as natural shank bones, nylon bones, hard rubber toys and pigs' feet or cow hooves are also excellent boredom chasers. Be very vigilant, though, in removing them when they become small enough for the Schnauzer to swallow whole. Schnauzers have been known to swallow small items whole when confronted with the prospect of losing the item to the owner or another dog.

Rawhide bones are not recommended, as they are too easily eaten and qualify as empty calories leading to overweight dogs. Plus, they can damage the leg and facial furnishings as well as cause intestinal blockage.

LEAD

A nylon lead is probably the best option, as it is the most resistant to puppy teeth should your pup take a liking to chewing on his lead. Of course, this is a habit that should be nipped in the bud, but, if your pup likes to chew on his lead, he has a very slim chance of being able to chew through the strong nylon. Nylon leads are also lightweight, which is good for a young Schnauzer who is just getting used to the idea of walking on a lead. For everyday walking and safety purposes, the nylon

TOYS, TOYS, TOYS!

With a big variety of dog toys available, and so many that look like they would be a lot of fun for a dog, be careful in your selection. It is amazing what a set of puppy teeth can do to an innocent-looking toy, so, obviously, safety is a major consideration. Be sure to choose the most durable products that you can find. Hard nylon bones and toys are a safe bet, and many of them are offered in different scents and flavours that will be sure to capture your dog's attention. It is always fun to play a game of catch with your dog, and there are balls and flying discs that are specially made to withstand dog teeth.

Purchase a light but sturdy lead for your Schnauzer. A quality lead will last many years of wear.

lead is a good choice. As your pup grows up and gets used to walking on the lead, you may want to purchase a flexible lead. These leads allow you to extend the length to give the dog a broader area to explore or to shorten the length to keep the dog near you. Of course, there are leads designed for training purposes and specially made leather harnesses, but these are not necessary for routine walks.

COLLAR

Your pup should get used to wearing a collar all the time since you will want to attach his ID tags to it; plus, you have to attach the

Your puppy's collar should fit snugly, but not tightly. Remember that his neck and coat will grow every day. Check the collar for tightness and safety.

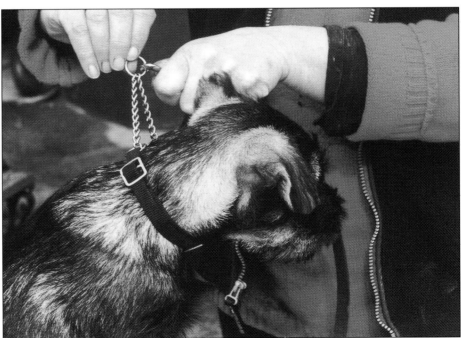

lead to something! A lightweight nylon collar is a good choice. Make certain that the collar fits snugly enough so that the pup cannot wriggle out of it, but is loose enough so that it will not be uncomfortably tight around the pup's neck. You should be able to fit a finger between the pup's neck and the collar. It may take some time for your pup to get used to wearing the collar, but soon he will not even notice that it is there. Choke collars are made for training, but should only be used by experienced handlers.

FOOD AND WATER BOWLS

Your pup will need two bowls, one for food and one for water. You may want two sets of bowls, one for indoors and one for outdoors, depending on where the dog will be fed and where he will be spending time. Stainless steel or sturdy plastic bowls are popular choices. Plastic bowls are more chewable, and dogs tend not to chew on the steel variety, which can be sterilised. It is important to buy sturdy bowls since anything is in danger of being chewed by puppy teeth and you do not want your dog to be constantly chewing apart his bowl (for his safety and for your purse!). Invest in a bowl stand to elevate your Schnauzer's bowls. This avoids the dog's having to crane its neck while eating, thus helping to ward off torsion (bloat).

Your local pet shop will have an assortment of food and water bowls from which you may choose the ones most suitable for your Schnauzer.

PHOTO COURTESY OF MIKKI PET PRODUCTS.

CLEANING SUPPLIES

Until a pup is house-trained, you will be doing a lot of cleaning. 'Accidents' will occur, which is acceptable in the beginning stages of toilet training because the puppy does not know any better. All you can do is be prepared to clean up any accidents as soon as they happen. Old rags, towels, newspapers and a safe disinfectant are good to have on hand.

BEYOND THE BASICS

The items previously discussed are the bare necessities. You will find out what else you need as you go along—grooming supplies, flea/tick protection, baby gates to partition a room, etc. These things will vary depending on your situation, but it is important that

you have everything you need to feed and make your Schnauzer comfortable in his first few days at home.

PUPPY-PROOFING YOUR HOME

Aside from making sure that your Schnauzer will be comfortable in your home, you also have to make sure that your home is safe for your Schnauzer. This means taking precautions that your pup will not get into anything he should not get into and that there is nothing within his reach that may harm him should he sniff it, chew it, inspect it, etc. This probably seems obvious but, while you are primarily concerned with your pup's safety, at the same time you do not want your belongings to be ruined. Breakables should be placed out of reach if your dog is to have full run of the house. If he is to be limited to certain places within the house, keep any potentially dangerous items in the 'off-limits' areas.

An electrical cord can pose a danger should the puppy decide to taste it—and who is going to convince a pup that it would not make a great chew toy? Cords should be fastened tightly against the wall. If your dog is going to spend time in a crate, make sure that there is nothing near his crate that he can reach if he sticks his curious little nose or paws through the openings. Just as you

CHOOSE AN APPROPRIATE COLLAR

The **BUCKLE COLLAR** is the standard collar used for everyday purposes. Be sure that you adjust the buckle on growing puppies. Check it every day. It can become too tight overnight! These collars can be made of leather or nylon. Attach your dog's identification tags to this collar.

The **CHOKE COLLAR** is constructed of highly polished steel so that it slides easily through the stainless steel loop. The idea is that the dog controls the pressure around its neck and he will stop pulling if the collar becomes uncomfortable.

The **HALTER** is for a trained dog that has to be restrained to prevent running away, chasing a cat and the like. Considered the most humane of all collars, it is frequently used on working dogs as well as smaller dogs for which collars are not comfortable.

should never be unsupervised, but a pup let loose in the garden will want to run and explore, and he should be granted that freedom. Do not let a fence give you a false sense of security; you would be surprised at how crafty (and persistent) a dog can be in working out how to dig under and squeeze his way through small holes, or to jump or climb over a fence.

Most Schnauzers are not climbers, but they are excellent jumpers and diggers. A four- to five-foot fence with 6 inches buried below the surface is usually sufficient to contain the Schnauzer...although some Schnauzers, being properly motivated, have gone over a 2-metre (6-foot) fence. Well-trained dogs can easily be contained with the lower-height fence. Many owners fence off their flower beds separately, as sometimes the Schnauzer does like to rearrange the garden. I know of one breeder that keeps all flowers in pots raised at least 18 inches so as not to be inadvertently 'watered' by the male Schnauzers.

FIRST TRIP TO THE VET
You have selected your puppy, and your home and family are ready. Now all you have to do is collect your Schnauzer from the breeder and the fun begins, right? Well...not so fast. Something else you need to plan is your pup's

TOXIC PLANTS
Many plants can be toxic to dogs. If you see your dog carrying a piece of vegetation in his mouth, approach him in a quiet, disinterested manner, avoid eye contact, pet him and gradually remove the plant from his mouth. Alternatively, offer him a treat and maybe he'll drop the plant on his own accord. Be sure no toxic plants are growing in your own garden.

would with a child, keep all household cleaners and chemicals where they cannot be reached.

It is also important to make sure that the outside of your home is safe. Of course, your puppy

first trip to the veterinary surgeon. Perhaps the breeder can recommend someone in the area who specialises in the schnauzer breeds, or maybe you know some other dog owners who can suggest a good vet. Either way, you should have an appointment arranged for your pup before you pick him up.

The pup's first visit will consist of an overall examination to make sure that the pup does not have any problems that are not apparent to you. The veterinary surgeon will also set up a schedule for the pup's vaccinations; the breeder will

PUPPY-PROOFING

Thoroughly puppy-proof your house before bringing your Schnauzer home. Never use cockroach or rodent poisons in any area accessible to the pup. Avoid the use of toilet cleaners. Most puppies are born with 'toilet sonar' and will take a drink if the lid is left open. Also keep the rubbish secured and out of reach.

NATURAL TOXINS

Examine your grass and garden landscaping before bringing your puppy home. Many varieties of plants have leaves, stems or flowers that are toxic if ingested, and you can depend on a curious puppy to investigate them. Ask your vet for information on poisonous plants or research them at your library.

inform you of which ones the pup has already received and the vet can continue from there.

INTRODUCTION TO THE FAMILY

Everyone in the house will be excited about the puppy's coming home and will want to pet him and play with him, but it is best to make the introduction low-key so as not to overwhelm the puppy. He is apprehensive already. It is the first time he has been separated from his mother and the breeder, and the ride to your home is likely to be the first time he has been in a car. The last thing you

ARE YOU A FIT OWNER?
If the breeder from whom you are buying a puppy asks you a lot of personal questions, do not be insulted. Such a breeder wants to be sure that you will be a fit provider for his puppy.

want to do is smother him, as this will only frighten him further. This is not to say that human contact is not extremely necessary at this stage, because this is the time when a connection between the pup and his human family is formed. Gentle petting and soothing words should help console him, as well as just putting him down and letting him explore on his own (under your watchful eye, of course).

The pup may approach the family members or may busy himself with exploring for a while. Gradually, each person should spend some time with the pup, one at a time, crouching down to get as close to the pup's level as possible, letting him sniff their hands and petting him gently. He definitely needs human attention and he needs to be touched—this is how to form an immediate bond. Just

remember that the pup is experiencing many things for the first time, at the same time. There are new people, new noises, new smells and new things to investigate, so be gentle, be affectionate and be as comforting as you can be.

PUP'S FIRST NIGHT HOME
You have travelled home with your new charge safely in his crate. He's been to the vet for a thorough check-up; he's been weighed, his papers have been examined and perhaps he's even been vaccinated and wormed as well. He's met (and licked!) the whole family, including the excited children and the less-than-happy cat. He's explored his area, his new bed, the garden and anywhere else he's been permitted. He's eaten his first meal at home and relieved himself in the proper place. He's heard lots of new sounds, smelled new friends and seen more of the outside world than ever before...and that was just

the first day! He's worn out and is ready for bed...or so you think!

It's puppy's first night home and you are ready to say 'Good night.' Keep in mind that this is his first night ever to be sleeping alone. His dam and littermates are no longer at paw's length and he's a bit scared, cold and lonely. Be reassuring to your new family member, but this is not the time to spoil him and give in to his inevitable whining.

Puppies whine. They whine to let others know where they are and hopefully to get company out of it. Place your pup in his new bed or crate in his designated area and close the door. Mercifully, he may fall asleep without a peep. When the inevitable occurs, however, ignore the whining—he is fine. Be strong and keep his interest in mind. Do not allow yourself to feel guilty and visit the pup. He will fall asleep eventually.

Many breeders recommend placing a piece of bedding from

HOW VACCINES WORK

If you've just bought a puppy, you surely know the importance of having your pup vaccinated, but do you understand how vaccines work? Vaccines contain the same bacteria or viruses that cause the disease you want to prevent, but they have been chemically modified so that they don't cause any harm. Instead, the vaccine causes your dog to produce antibodies that fight the harmful bacteria. Thus, if your dog is exposed to the disease in the future, the antibodies will destroy the viruses or bacteria.

CHEMICAL TOXINS

Scour your garage for potential puppy dangers. Remove weed killers, pesticides and antifreeze materials. Antifreeze is highly toxic and even a few drops can kill a puppy or adult dog. The sweet taste attracts the animal, who will quickly consume it from the floor or curbside.

the pup's former home in his new bed so that he recognises and is comforted by the scent of his littermates. Others still advise placing a hot water bottle in the bed for warmth. The latter may be a good idea provided the pup doesn't attempt to suckle—he'll get good and wet, and may not fall asleep so fast.

Puppy's first night can be somewhat stressful for both the pup and his new family. Remember that you are setting the

MANNERS MATTER

During the socialisation process, a puppy should meet people, experience different environments and definitely be exposed to other canines. Through playing and interacting with other dogs, your puppy will learn lessons, ranging from controlling the pressure of his jaws by biting his littermates to the inner-workings of the canine pack that he will apply to his human relationships for the rest of his life. That is why removing a puppy from its litter too early (before eight weeks) can be detrimental to the pup's development.

PREVENTING PUPPY PROBLEMS

SOCIALISATION

Now that you have done all of the preparatory work and have helped your pup get accustomed to his new home and family, it is about time for you to have some fun! Socialising your Schnauzer pup gives you the opportunity to show off your new friend, and your pup gets to reap the benefits of being an adorable furry creature that people will want to pet and, in general, think is absolutely precious!

Besides getting to know his new family, your puppy should be exposed to other people, animals and situations. This will help him become well adjusted as he grows up and less prone to being timid or fearful of the new things he will encounter. Of course, he must not come into close contact with dogs you don't know well until his course of injections is fully complete.

Your pup's socialisation began with the breeder, but now it is your responsibility to continue it. The socialisation he receives until the age of 12 weeks is the most critical, as this is the time when he forms his impressions of the outside world. Be especially careful during the eight-to-ten-week-old period, also known as the fear period. The interaction he receives during this time should

tone of night-time at your house. Unless you want to play with your pup every night at 10 p.m., midnight and 2 a.m., don't initiate the habit. Your family will thank you, and so will your pup!

MEET THE WORLD

Thorough socialisation includes not only meeting new people but also being introduced to new experiences such as riding in the car, having his coat brushed, hearing the television, walking in a crowd—the list is endless. The more your pup experiences, and the more positive the experiences are, the less of a shock and the less frightening it will be for your pup to encounter new things.

for example, that is great—children and pups most often make great companions. However, sometimes an excited child can unintentionally handle a pup too roughly, or an overzealous pup can playfully nip a little too hard. You want to make socialisation experiences positive ones. What a pup learns during this very formative stage will affect his attitude toward future encounters. You want your dog to be comfortable around everyone. A pup that

be gentle and reassuring. Lack of socialisation, and/or negative experiences during the socialisation period, can manifest itself in fear and aggression as the dog grows up. Your puppy needs lots of positive interaction, which of course includes human contact, affection, handling and exposure to other animals.

Once your pup has received his necessary vaccinations, feel free to take him out and about (on his lead, of course). Walk him around the neighbourhood, take him on your daily errands, let people pet him, let him meet other dogs and pets, etc. Puppies do not have to try to make friends; there will be no shortage of people who will want to introduce themselves. Just make sure that you carefully supervise each meeting. If the neighbourhood children want to say hello,

PROPER SOCIALISATION

The socialisation period for puppies is from age 8 to 16 weeks. This is the time when puppies need to leave their birth family and take up residence with their new owners, where they will meet many new people, other pets, etc. Failure to be adequately socialised can cause the dog to grow up fearing others and being shy and unfriendly due to a lack of self-confidence.

has a bad experience with a child may grow up to be a dog that is shy around or aggressive toward children.

CONSISTENCY IN TRAINING

Dogs, being pack animals, naturally need a leader, or else they try to establish dominance in their packs. When you welcome a dog into your family, the choice of who becomes the leader and who becomes the 'pack' is entirely up to you! Your pup's intuitive quest for dominance, coupled with the fact that it is nearly impossible to look at an adorable Schnauzer pup with his little bearded face and not cave in, give the pup almost an unfair advantage in getting the upper hand! A pup will definitely test the waters to see what he can and cannot do.

Do not give in to those adorable whiskers—stand your ground when it comes to disciplining the pup and make sure that all family members do the same. It will only confuse the pup if Mother tells him to get off the sofa when he is used to sitting up there with Father to watch the nightly news. Avoid discrepancies by having all members of the household decide on the rules before the pup even comes home...and be consistent in enforcing them! Early training shapes the dog's personality, so you cannot be unclear in what you expect.

COMMON PUPPY PROBLEMS

The best way to prevent puppy problems is to be proactive in stopping an undesirable behaviour as soon as it starts. The old saying 'You can't teach an old dog new tricks' does not necessarily hold true, but it is true that it is much easier to discourage bad behaviour in a young developing pup than to wait until the pup's bad behaviour becomes the adult dog's bad habit. There are some problems that are especially prevalent in puppies as they develop.

NIPPING

As puppies start to teethe, they feel the need to sink their teeth into anything available...unfortunately, that usually includes your fingers, arms, hair and toes. You may find this behaviour cute for the first *five seconds*...until you feel just how sharp those puppy teeth are. Nipping is something you want to discourage immediately and consistently with a firm 'No!' (or whatever number of firm 'Nos' it takes for him to understand that you mean business). Then, replace your finger with an appropriate chew toy. While this behaviour is merely annoying when the dog is young, it can become dangerous as your Schnauzer's adult teeth grow in and his jaws develop, and he continues to think it is okay to gnaw on human appendages. Your

Schnauzer does not mean any harm with a friendly nip, but he also does not know his own rat-crushing strength.

CRYING/WHINING

Your pup will often cry, whine, whimper, howl or make some type of commotion when he is left alone. This is basically his way of calling out for attention to make sure that you know he is there and that you have not forgotten about him. Your puppy feels insecure when he is left alone, when you are out of the house and he is in his crate or when you are in another part of the house and he cannot see you. The noise he is making is an expression of the anxiety he feels at being alone, so he needs to be taught that being alone is okay. You are not actually training the dog to stop making noise; rather, you are training him to feel comfortable when he is alone and thus removing the need for him to make the noise.

This is where the crate with cosy bedding and a toy comes in handy. You want to know that your pup is safe when you are not there to supervise, and you know that he will be safe in his crate rather than roaming freely about the house. In order for the pup to stay in his crate without making a fuss, he first needs to be comfortable in his crate. On that note, it is extremely important that the

Love, care and affection from the start create the special lifelong bond between a dog and his family.

crate is never used as a form of punishment; this will cause the pup to view the crate as a negative place, rather than as a place of his own for safety and retreat.

Accustom the pup to the crate in short, gradually increasing time intervals in which you put him in the crate, maybe with a treat, and stay in the room with him. If he cries or makes a fuss, do not go to him, but stay in his sight. Gradually he will realise that staying in his crate is all right without your help, and it will not be so traumatic for him when you are not around. You may want to leave the radio on softly when you leave the house; the sound of human voices may be comforting to him.

PUPPY PROBLEMS

The majority of problems that are commonly seen in young pups will disappear as your dog gets older. However, how you deal with problems when he is young will determine how he reacts to discipline as an adult dog.

Your Schnauzer
will soon become
a part of your
everyday routine.
A canine
companion wants
to share in as
much of your day
as possible.

DIETARY AND FEEDING CONSIDERATIONS

Today the choices of food for your Schnauzer are many and varied. There are simply dozens of brands of food in all sorts of flavours and textures, ranging from puppy diets to those for seniors. There are even hypoallergenic and low-calorie diets available. Because your Schnauzer's food has a bearing on coat, health and temperament, it is essential that the most suitable diet is selected for a Schnauzer of his age. It is fair to say, however, that even experienced owners can be perplexed by the enormous range of foods available. Only understanding what is best for your dog will help you reach an informed decision.

Dog foods are produced in three basic types: dried, semi-moist and tinned. Dried foods are useful for the cost-conscious, for overall they tend to be less expensive than semi-moist or tinned foods. Dried foods also contain the least fat and the most preservatives. In general, tinned foods are made up of 60–70 percent water, while semi-moist

ones often contain so much sugar that they are perhaps the least preferred by owners, even though their dogs seem to like them.

When selecting your dog's diet, three stages of development must be considered: the puppy stage, the adult stage and the senior or veteran stage.

FEEDING TIP

You must store your dried dog food carefully. Open packages of dog food quickly lose their vitamin value, usually within 90 days of being opened. Mould spores and vermin could also contaminate the food.

FEEDING TIPS

Dog food must be at room temperature, neither too hot nor too cold. Fresh water, changed daily and served in a clean bowl, is mandatory, especially when feeding dried food.

Never feed your dog from the table while you are eating, and never feed your dog leftovers from your own meal. They usually contain too much fat and too much seasoning.

Dogs must chew their food. Hard pellets are excellent; soups and slurries are to be avoided.

Don't add leftovers or any extras to normal dog food. The normal food is usually balanced, and adding something extra destroys the balance.

Except for age-related changes, dogs do not require dietary variations. They can be fed the same diet, day after day, without becoming ill.

PUPPY STAGE

Puppies instinctively want to suck milk from their mother's teats; a normal puppy will exhibit this behaviour just a few moments following birth. If puppies do not attempt to suckle within the first half-hour or so, they should be encouraged to do so by placing them on the nipples, having selected ones with plenty of milk. This early milk supply is important in providing the essential colostrum, which protects the puppies during the first eight to ten weeks of their lives. Although a mother's milk is much better than any milk formula, despite there being some excellent ones available, if the puppies do not feed, the breeder will have to feed them by hand. For those with less experience, advice from a veterinary surgeon is important so that not only the right quantity of milk is fed but also that of correct quality, fed at suitably frequent intervals, usually every two hours during the first few days of life.

Puppies should be allowed to nurse from their mothers for about the first six weeks, although, starting around the third or fourth week, the breeder will begin to introduce small portions of suitable solid food. Most breeders like to alternate milk and meat meals initially, building up to weaning time.

By the time the puppies are seven or a maximum of eight weeks old, they should be fully weaned and fed solely on a proprietary puppy food. Selection of the most suitable, good-quality diet at this time is essential, for a puppy's fastest growth rate is during the first year of life. Veterinary surgeons are usually able to offer advice in this regard and, although the frequency of meals will be reduced over time, only when a young dog has reached the age of about eight to ten months should an adult diet be fed. One exception to this rule is for a puppy that is too hyperactive and not getting enough exercise; this pup can be put on a good-quality adult food that contains fewer calories and less energy-producing fat and protein.

Puppy and junior diets should be well balanced for the needs of your dog so that, except in certain circumstances, additional vitamins, minerals and proteins will not be required.

ADULT DIETS

In general, the diet of a Schnauzer can be changed to an adult one at about eight to ten months of age, as by this age the dog will have reached most of its mature height and weight. Again you should rely upon your veterinary surgeon or dietary specialist to recommend an acceptable maintenance diet. Major dog food

FOOD PREFERENCE

Selecting the best dried dog food is difficult. There is no majority consensus among veterinary scientists as to the value of nutrient analyses (protein, fat, fibre, moisture, ash, cholesterol, minerals, etc.). All agree that feeding trials are what matter, but you also have to consider the individual dog. The dog's weight, age and activity level, and what pleases his taste, all must be considered. It is probably best to take the advice of your veterinary surgeon. Every dog's dietary requirements vary, even during the lifetime of a particular dog.

If your dog is fed a good dried food, it does not require supplements of meat or vegetables. Dogs do appreciate a little variety in their diets, so you may choose to stay with the same brand but vary the flavour. Alternatively, you may wish to add a little flavoured stock to give a difference to the taste.

Adult and puppy Schnauzers should have different diets, though pups will try to eat anything that their dam does.

manufacturers specialise in this type of food, and it is merely necessary for you to select the one best suited to your dog's needs. Active dogs may have different requirements than sedate dogs.

The Schnauzer is usually not a picky eater. Most eat their food like they were four-legged hoovers. The amount of food varies with each dog, ranging from one-and-a-half-cups a day for an inactive 'couch potato' to three to four cups a day for an extremely active dog. The average, which works for most adult Schnauzers, is one cup twice a day.

Most Schnauzers seem to have stomachs of cast iron and can take changes in diet easily. Sometimes you will find one with a very sensitive stomach that has to be introduced to new food very slowly. A lot of them, when given the chance, will relish the opportunity to eat new grass. I had one that had a passion for

Zinnia plants. Needless to say, grass and Zinnia plants are not recommended diets.

SENIOR DIETS
The Schnauzer ages very well and is a very 'youthful' dog for much longer than many other breeds their size. Whereas many breeds are started on 'senior' food at six or seven years of age, most Schnauzer breeders do not put them on senior food until nine or ten years of age. At this time, a change in diet becomes warranted. As dogs get older, their metabolism changes. The older dog usually exercises less, moves more slowly and sleeps more. This change in lifestyle and physiological performance

GRAIN-BASED DIETS
Some less expensive dog foods are based on grains and other plant proteins. While these products may appear to be attractively priced, many breeders prefer a diet based on animal proteins and believe that they are more conducive to your dog's health. Many grain-based diets rely on soy protein, which may cause flatulence (passing gas).

There are many cases, however, when your dog might require a special diet. These special require-ments should only be recommended by your veterinary surgeon.

TIPPING THE SCALES

Good nutrition is vital to your dog's health, but many people end up over-feeding or giving unnecessary supplements. Here are some common doggie diet don'ts:

- Adding milk, yoghurt and cheese to your dog's diet may seem like a good idea for coat and skin care, but dairy products are very fattening and can cause indigestion.
- Diets high in fat will not cause heart attacks in dogs but will certainly cause your dog to gain weight.
- Most importantly, don't assume your dog will simply stop eating once he doesn't need any more food. Given the chance, he will eat you out of house and home!

a change in feeding schedule to give smaller portions that are more easily digested. There is no single best diet for every older dog. While many dogs do well on light or senior diets, other dogs do better on puppy diets or other special premium diets such as lamb and rice. Be sensitive to your senior Schnauzer's diet, as this will help control other problems that may arise with your old friend.

WATER

Just as your dog needs proper nutrition from his food, water is an essential 'nutrient' as well. Water keeps the dog's body properly hydrated and promotes normal function of the body's systems. During house-training it

requires some altering of the dog's feeding.

Since changes due to ageing take place slowly, they might not be recognisable. What is easily recognisable is weight gain. By continuing to feed your dog an adult-maintenance diet when it is slowing down metabolically, your dog will gain weight. Obesity in an older dog compounds the health problems that may accompany old age.

As your dog gets older, few of his organs function up to par. The kidneys slow down and the intestines become less efficient. These age-related factors are best handled with a change in diet and

CHANGE IN DIET

As your dog's caretaker, you know the importance of keeping his diet consistent, but sometimes when you run out of food or if you're on holiday, you have to make a change quickly. Some dogs will experience digestive problems, but most will not. If you are planning on changing your dog's menu, do so gradually to ensure that your dog will not have any problems. Over a period of two to three days, slowly add some new food to your dog's old food, increasing the percentage of new food each day.

DRINK, DRANK, DRUNK— MAKE IT A DOUBLE

In both humans and dogs, as well as most living organisms, water forms the major part of nearly every body tissue. Naturally, we take water for granted, but without it, life as we know it would cease.

For dogs, water is needed to keep their bodies functioning biochemically. Additionally, water is needed to replace the water lost while panting. Unlike humans, who are able to sweat to dissipate heat, dogs must pant to cool down, thereby losing the vital water from their bodies needed to regulate their body temperatures. Humans lose electrolyte-containing products and other body-fluid components through sweating; dogs do not lose anything except water.

Water is essential always, but especially so when the weather is hot or humid or when your dog is exercising or working vigorously.

is necessary to keep an eye on how much water your Schnauzer is drinking, but once he is reliably trained he should have access to clean fresh water at all times, especially if you feed dried food. Make certain that the dog's water bowl is clean, and change the water often.

EXERCISE

The amount of exercise that a Schnauzer needs to be kept in top condition depends very much on the individual dog, but the breed as a whole does require moderate exercise. A Schnauzer living in a flat needs a minimum of three brisk walks of one to two miles per day to be kept in top physical condition. In a kennel or house environment, some Schnauzers are self-motivated exercisers and will keep constantly moving, using any excuse available, especially if they have a playmate. On the other hand, there is the occasional 'couch potato' that must be coaxed to exercise. If you

DO DOGS HAVE TASTE BUDS?

Watching a dog 'wolf' or gobble his food, seemingly without chewing, leads an owner to wonder whether their dogs can taste anything. Yes, dogs have taste buds, with sensory perception of sweet, salty and sour. Puppies are born with fully mature taste buds.

What are you feeding your dog?

Read the label on your dog food. Many dog foods only advise what 50—55% of the contents are, leaving the other 45% in doubt.

Calcium 1.3%
Fatty Acids 1.6%
Crude Fibre 4.6%
Moisture 11%
Crude Fat 14%
Crude Protein 22%
45.5% ? ? ?

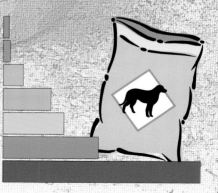

do have a such a dog, a minimum of two very brisk half-hour daily walks is strongly recommended.

Play sessions in the garden and letting the dog run free in the garden under your supervision also are sufficient forms of exercise for the Schnauzer. Fetching games can be played indoors or out; these are excellent for giving your dog active play that he will enjoy. Chasing things that move comes naturally to dogs of all breeds. When your Schnauzer runs after the ball or object, praise him for picking it up and encourage him to bring it back to you for another

> **THE CANINE GOURMET**
> Your dog does not prefer a fresh bone. Indeed, he wants it properly aged and, if given such a treat indoors, he is more likely to try to bury it in the carpet than he is to settle in for a good chew! If you have a garden, give him such delicacies outside and guide him to a place suitable for his 'bone yard.' He will carefully place the treasure in its earthy vault and seemingly forget about it. Trust me, his seeming distaste or lack of thanks for your thoughtfulness is not that at all. He will return in a few days to inspect the bone, perhaps to re-bury it, and when it is just right, he will relish it as much as you do that cooked-to-perfection steak. If he is in a concrete or bricked kennel run, he will be especially frustrated at the hopelessness of the situation. He will vacillate between ignoring it completely, giving it a few licks to speed the curing process with saliva and trying to hide it behind the water bowl! When the bone has aged a bit, he will set to work on it.

Exercise is good for owner and Schnauzer alike. A flexible lead is useful once the dog has been trained to heel using a traditional lead.

> **EXERCISE CAUTION**
> Never tie a dog out to a post or tree, thinking that you are giving him exercise. This will only serve to increase aggression in the dog; with a breed that is naturally protective, tying the dog out can make the him mean.

throw. Never go to the object and pick it up yourself, or you'll soon find that you are the one retrieving the objects rather than the dog!

If you choose to play games outdoors, you must have a securely fenced-in garden and/or have the dog attached to at least a 25-foot light line for security. You want your Schnauzer to run, but not run away!

GROOMING EQUIPMENT

How much grooming equipment you purchase will depend on how much grooming you are going to do. Here are some basics:

- Stiff bristle brush
- Slicker brush
- Metal comb
- Scissors
- Blaster
- Rubber mat
- Dog shampoo
- Spray hose attachment
- Ear cleaner
- Cotton wipes
- Towels
- Stripping knife (optional)
- Nail clippers
- Electric clipper (optional)

Bear in mind that an overweight dog should never be suddenly over-exercised; instead he should be encouraged to increase exercise slowly. Remember that not only is exercise essential to keep the dog's body fit, it is essential to his mental well-being. A bored dog will find something to do, which often manifests itself in some type of destructive behaviour. In this sense, exercise is essential for the owner's mental well-being as well!

GROOMING THE SCHNAUZER

The 'jacket' on the Schnauzer is a relatively high-maintenance job if you are planning to show your

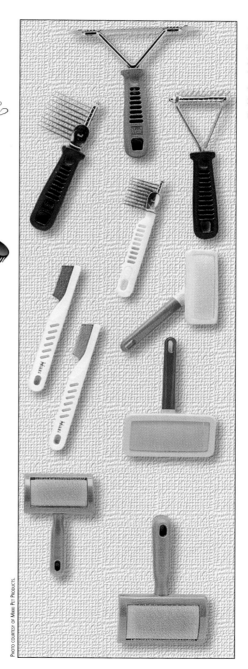

Your local pet shop will have grooming tools with which you can keep your Schnauzer's coat in good condition.

PHOTO COURTESY OF MIKKI PET PRODUCTS.

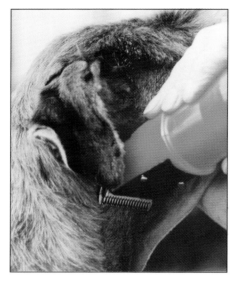

Although not the preferred method by Schnauzer people, machine-clipping is a satisfactory method for pet dogs and retired show dogs. Electric clipping causes the coat to lose its coarseness and coloration.

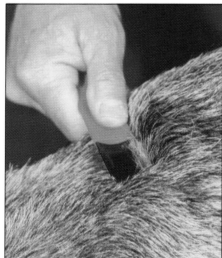

More time-intensive hand-stripping is the preferred method of maintaining a Schnauzer's coat. Ask a professional groomer or your breeder how to properly use a stripping knife.

the local grooming parlour and have the body coat machine-clipped. The very distinctive leg furnishings, beard and eyebrows of the Schnauzer do not shed like the jacket. They continue to grow and are always hand-scissored when the jacket is clipped. The Schnauzer groomed this way requires a trip to the parlour every six to eight weeks. This method of grooming is much quicker, easier on the dog and most certainly easier on the purse.

Most breeders routinely machine-clip their old-timers that are no longer being shown. The one big drawback to this method is that in most cases the coat becomes much softer over the years. The characteristic pepper and salt coloration gradually fades out and turns to a solid grey. The black dogs gradually lose the shine to their coats, with some developing a brownish tinge to the coat.

The proper method of maintaining the Schnauzer coat is to hand-strip the jacket. This is the way that the jacket is maintained in show dogs. If you choose this option, you must either learn how to hand-strip (pluck out) the harsh wiry outer topcoat yourself, or find an experienced fellow owner, handler or breeder who is willing to teach you—or better yet, do it for you! Hand-stripping requires a minimum of twice-a-week maintenance in a dog being actively shown, or approximately two or three times a year, depending on the harshness of the

dog. For the average Schnauzer kept strictly as a companion and family pet, there are two options for maintaining the jacket. The easiest option is to take the dog to

coat, for the well-maintained pet. The furnishings (once again, depending on the texture) of the dog being maintained this way can either be done by hand with scissors or by hand-plucking only the longest hairs to tidy up the legs.

Hand-stripping or plucking of the jacket is the removal of the dead hair from the hair shaft. The hair is not cut. This method keeps the desirable hard, wiry texture of the jacket, which is one of the Schnauzer's outstanding characteristics. The dog must be maintained in this fashion if he is being shown in the conformation ring, as the texture of the jacket is a very major consideration. In some parts of the world, breeders, in an attempt to make a prettier dog with more profuse leg and beard furnishings, do not pay as much attention to texture of the outer coat as they should.

These dogs are particularly hard to hand-strip. A very strong word of warning: Be very careful when you first talk to a local all-breed groomer about trimming your Schnauzer. Be very specific and request that the dog be 'hand-stripped' or 'plucked' if that is the method by which you wish your dog to be maintained. If you do not specifically use this terminology, you could return later to find that your dog has been machine-stripped (clipped) of ALL hair, including that on the

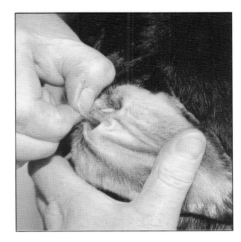

Long hairs growing out of the ear can be easily plucked out.

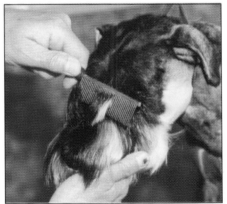

A strong steel-toothed comb is very useful on facial hairs, especially around the muzzle to prevent food particles from accumulating.

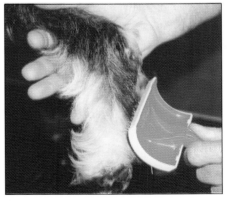

A slicker brush may be used for the hair on the Schnauzer's feet.

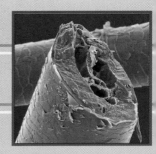

Normal hairs of a dog enlarged 200 times original size. The cuticle (outer covering) is clean and healthy. Unlike human hair that grows from the base, a dog's hair also grows from the end. Damaged hairs and split ends, illustrated above.

muzzle, eyes and legs! And that makes for a very embarrassed and sad-looking Schnauzer.

Whichever method is used to maintain the coat, a daily washing and combing of the beard is required to prevent build-up of food particles and to prevent doggy odours. The beard and leg furnishings should be combed out two or three times a week to prevent mats from forming. A brushing of the body coat with a stiff bristle brush twice a week will keep the skin and body coat in excellent condition and free of odours and dirt.

Bathing the Schnauzer is not necessary unless your dog decides to revert to his wild canine instincts of rolling in some horrible smelly mess that he considers to be perfume of the gods. Mary Moore (Odivane kennels) tells the story of six of her dogs, when out for a walk, jumping into a black muck ditch. When she pulled them out, all covered in the black muck, they didn't even recognise each other and at once started a fight. Needless to say, all dogs promptly went home and had a good bath.

BATHING

Brush your Schnauzer thoroughly before wetting his coat. This will get rid of most mats and tangles, which are harder to remove when the coat is wet. Make certain that your dog has a good non-slip

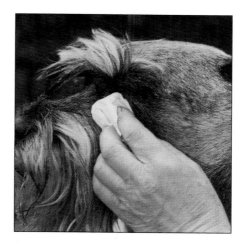

Tear stains are easily removed with a soft cloth and suitable tear-stain remover.

Your Schnauzer's teeth should be sparkling white and clean.

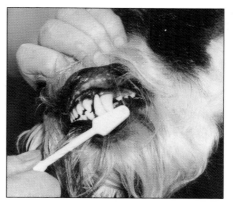

Use a suitable dog toothpaste and toothbrush when caring for your Schnauzer's teeth.

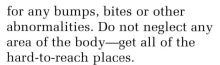

surface on which to stand. Begin by wetting the dog's coat, checking the water temperature to make sure that it is neither too hot nor too cold. A shower or hose attachment is necessary for thoroughly wetting and rinsing the coat.

Next, apply shampoo to the dog's coat and work it into a good lather. Wash the head last, as you do not want shampoo to drip into the dog's eyes while you are washing the rest of his body. You should use only a shampoo that is made for dogs. Do not use a product made for human hair. Work the shampoo all the way down to the skin. You can use this opportunity to check the skin

for any bumps, bites or other abnormalities. Do not neglect any area of the body—get all of the hard-to-reach places.

Once the dog has been thoroughly shampooed, he requires an equally thorough rinsing. Shampoo left in the coat can be irritating to the dog's skin. Protect his eyes from the shampoo by shielding them with your hand and directing the flow of water in the opposite direction. You should also avoid getting water in the ear canal. Be prepared for your dog to shake out his coat— you might want to stand back, but make sure you have an hold on the dog to keep him from running through the house.

BATHING BEAUTY

Once you are sure that the dog is thoroughly rinsed, squeeze the excess water out of his coat with your hand and dry him with a heavy towel. You may choose to use a blaster on his coat or just let it dry naturally. In cold weather, never allow your dog outside with a wet coat.

There are 'dry bath' products on the market, which are sprays and powders intended for spot cleaning, that can be used between regular baths if necessary. They are not substitutes for regular baths, but they are easy to use for touch-ups as they do not require rinsing.

TEETH

Although the Schnauzer is blessed with strong teeth and gums, many dogs will develop plaque on their teeth as they grow older if given a lot of soft food. By brushing the teeth weekly and making sure the dog has a variety of hard objects to chew on, trips to the veterinary clinic for major tooth cleanings can be greatly reduced.

Introduce your pup to weekly tooth-brushing as a routine part of grooming. Brushing can be done with a doggy toothbrush, a soft baby toothbrush or several layers of gauze wrapped around your finger. You can use a doggy toothpaste, or just moisten the brush or gauze with plain water and lightly scrub each tooth on the top and bottom jaws to remove the plaque.

Ear Cleaning

The ears should be kept clean with a cotton wipe and ear powder made especially for dogs. Do not probe into the ear canal with a cotton bud, as this can cause injury. Be on the lookout for any signs of infection or ear-mite infestation. If your Schnauzer has been shaking his head or scratching at his ears frequently, this usually indicates a problem. If the dog's ears have an unusual odour, this is a sure sign of mite infestation or infection, and a signal to have his ears checked by the veterinary surgeon.

Nail Clipping

Your Schnauzer should be accustomed to having his nails trimmed at an early age since nail clipping will be part of your maintenance routine throughout his life. Not only does it look nicer, but long nails can scratch someone unintentionally. Also, a long nail has a better chance of ripping and bleeding, or causing the feet to spread. A good rule of thumb is that if you can hear your dog's nails' clicking on the floor when he walks, his nails are too long.

Before you start cutting, make sure you can identify the 'quick' in each nail. The quick is a blood

PEDICURE TIP

A dog that spends a lot of time outside on a hard surface, such as cement or pavement, will have his nails naturally worn down and may not need to have them trimmed as often, except maybe in the colder months when he is not outside as much. Regardless, it is best to get your dog accustomed to the nail-trimming procedure at an early age so that he is used to it. Some dogs are especially sensitive about having their feet touched, but if a dog has experienced it since puppyhood, it should not bother him.

vessel that runs through the centre of each nail and grows rather close to the end. The quick will bleed if accidentally cut, which will be quite painful for the dog, as it contains nerve endings. Keep some type of clotting agent on

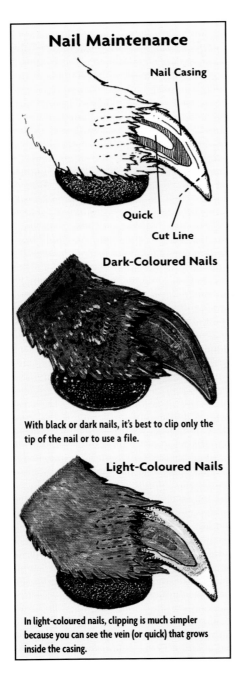

Nail Maintenance

Nail Casing

Quick

Cut Line

Dark-Coloured Nails

With black or dark nails, it's best to clip only the tip of the nail or to use a file.

Light-Coloured Nails

In light-coloured nails, clipping is much simpler because you can see the vein (or quick) that grows inside the casing.

hand, such as a styptic pencil or styptic powder (the type used for shaving). This will stop the bleeding quickly when applied to the end of the cut nail. Do not panic if you cut the quick, just stop the bleeding and talk soothingly to your dog. Once he has calmed down, move on to the next nail. It is better to clip a little at a time with the Schnauzer's dark nails.

Hold your pup steady as you begin trimming his nails; you do not want him to make any sudden movements or run away. Talk to him soothingly and stroke him as you clip. Holding his foot in your hand, simply take off the end of each nail with one swift clip. You should purchase nail clippers that are made for use on dogs; you can probably find them wherever you buy pet or grooming supplies.

TRAVELLING WITH YOUR DOG

CAR TRAVEL

You should accustom your Schnauzer to riding in a car at an early age. You may or may not take him in the car often, but at the very least he will need to go to the vet and you do not want these trips to be traumatic for the puppy or troublesome for you. The safest way for a pup to ride in the car is in his crate. If he uses a crate in the house, you can use the same crate for travel. Put the pup in the crate and see how he reacts. If he seems uneasy, you can have a passenger hold him on his lap while you drive.

An option for car travel more suited to adult dogs is a specially made safety harness, which straps the dog in much like a seat belt. A dividing gate for your vehicle, which will confine your Schnauzer to the rear of a van or truck, is also a viable choice for the adult. Do not let the dog roam loose in the vehicle—this is very dangerous! If you should stop short, your dog can be thrown and injured. If the dog starts climbing on you and pestering you while you are driving, you will not be able to concentrate on the road. It is an unsafe situation for everyone—human and canine.

For long trips, be prepared to stop to let the dog relieve himself. Take with you whatever you need to clean up after him, including some paper kitchen towels and perhaps some old towelling for use should he have a toileting accident in the car or suffer from travel sickness.

AIR TRAVEL

While it is possible to take a dog on a flight within Britain, this is fairly unusual and advance permission is always required. The dog will be required to travel in a fibreglass crate and you should always check in advance with the airline regarding specific requirements. To help put the dog

at ease, give him one of his favourite toys in the crate. Do not feed the dog for several hours before checking in, in order to minimise his need to relieve himself. However, certain regulations specify that water must always be made available to the dog in the crate.

Make sure that your dog is

MOTION SICKNESS

*If life is a motorway...*your dog may not want to come along for the ride! Some dogs experience motion sickness in cars that leads to excessive salivation and even vomiting. In most cases, your dog will fare better in the familiar, safe confines of his crate. To desensitise your dog, try going on several short jaunts before trying a long trip. If your dog experiences distress when riding in the vehicle, drive with him only when absolutely necessary, and do not feed him or give him water before you go.

properly identified and that your contact information appears on his ID tags and on his crate. Except for very small pets, animals travel in a different area of the plane than human passengers, so every rule must be strictly followed so as to prevent the risk of getting separated from your Schnauzer.

HOLIDAYS AND BOARDING

So you want to take a family holiday—and you want to include all members of the family. You would probably make arrangements for accommodation ahead of time anyway, but this is especially important when travelling with a dog. You do not want to make an overnight stop at the only place around for miles, only to find out that they do not allow dogs. Also, you do not want to reserve a place for your family without confirming that you are travelling with a dog, because, if it is against their policy, you may end up without a place to stay.

Alternatively, if you are travelling and choose not to bring your Schnauzer, you will have to make arrangements for him while you are away. Some options are to take him to a neighbour's house to stay while you are gone, to have a trusted neighbour pop in often or stay at your house or to bring your dog to a reputable boarding kennel. If you choose to board him at a kennel, you should visit in advance to see the facilities

provided and where the dogs are kept. Are the dogs' areas spacious and kept clean? Talk to some of the employees and see how they treat the dogs—do they spend time with the dogs, play with them, exercise them, etc.? Also find out the kennel's policy on vaccinations and what they require. This is for all of the dogs' safety, since there is a greater risk of diseases being passed from dog to dog when dogs are kept together.

TRAVEL TIP

The most extensive travel you do with your dog may be limited to trips to the veterinary surgeon's office—or you may decide to bring him along for long distances when the family goes on holiday. Whichever the case, it is important to consider your dog's safety while travelling.

CONSIDERATIONS ABOUT BOARDING

Will your dog be exercised at least twice a day? How often during the day will the staff keep him company? Does the kennel provide a clean and secure environment? These are some of the questions you should consider when choosing a boarding kennel.

Likewise, if the staff asks you a lot of questions, this is a good sign. They need to know your dog's personality and temperament, health record, special requirements and what commands he has learned. Above all, follow your instincts. If you have a bad feeling about a kennel, even if a friend has recommended it, don't put your dog in its care.

IDENTIFICATION

Your Schnauzer is your valued companion and friend. That is why you always keep a close eye on him and you have made sure that he cannot escape from the garden or wriggle out of his collar and run away from you. However, accidents can happen and there may come a time when your dog unexpectedly becomes separated from you. If this unfortunate event should occur, the first thing on your mind will be finding him. Proper identification, including an ID tag, a tattoo and possibly a microchip, will increase the chances of his being returned to you safely and quickly.

Versatile and agile, Schnauzers can be trained to a high degree of excellence in obedience and agility competition. This is Am Ch Pepper Tree Bel Air Austin, CD, OA, OAJ, clearing the high jump.

Training Your
SCHNAUZER

As your Schnauzer puppy grows up, you will have to make some decisions about the education of your new charge. This highly intelligent dog, if left in charge of his own upbringing, will very quickly take over the day-to-day running of your household. It is recommended that every Schnauzer have some form of formal obedience training. This is almost mandatory for the first-time Schnauzer owner, as the first two years of a Schnauzer's life can be very trying, even to the seasoned Schnauzer owner.

Schnauzers constantly try new ways to test the limits with their owners. Sometimes it is amusing, and sometimes anything but amusing. Some Schnauzers have an amazing sense of humour, while others are very serious about everything in their lives. Because of the breed's superior intelligence, the Schnauzer is not the dog for everyone. They can be wilfully strong-minded individuals, more than some owners can deal with.

The Schnauzer needs consistent firm leadership, but never by harsh or overbearing methods. The Schnauzer will work readily and happily if praised for positive behaviour; punishment for bad behaviour never impresses the Schnauzer. An owner must have the proverbial 'patience of Job' and an equally strong iron will as

REAP THE REWARDS

If you start with a normal, healthy dog and give him time, patience and some carefully executed lessons, you will reap the rewards of that training for the life of the dog. And what a life it will be! The two of you will find immeasurable pleasure in the companionship you have built together with love, respect and understanding.

the dog he is training. You, as the owner, must establish your authority as 'pack leader,' or the Schnauzer will claim the title for himself.

Schnauzers are very quick to pick up new commands if explained to them in a logical way. Never assume that because the Schnauzer is so smart that you can skip a few steps in the learning process. Once a command is learned, a Schnauzer will never forget it. Of course, some clever Schnauzers will work out variations or test their owners to make sure the command is a mandatory one. Trainers and owners must make sure that each command is taught properly the first time or else errors will haunt them forever, especially if the owner plans to work in competition or performance events with his dog.

One very important note is that the breed on the whole will not tolerate excessive repetition like some other breeds do. Boredom is a word not in the Schnauzer's vocabulary.

Those involved with teaching dog obedience and counselling owners about their dogs' behaviour have discovered some interesting facts about dog ownership. For example, training dogs when they are puppies results in the highest rate of success in developing well-mannered and well-adjusted adult dogs. Training an older dog, from six months to six years of age, can produce almost equal results providing that the owner accepts the dog's slower rate of learning capability and is willing to work patiently to help the dog succeed at developing to his fullest potential. Unfortunately, many owners of untrained adult dogs lack the patience factor, so they do not persist until their dogs are successful at learning particular behaviours.

The recommended ideal age to train a pup varies from trainer to trainer. Unfortunately, some trainers do not know how to work with the very young puppies, leaving new owners to fend for themselves until the pup is six to eight months of age. This, I feel, is too late for the average novice owner of the Schnauzer. I am a firm believer in starting the owner and his pup in gentle training as early as possible. The earlier you start, the more you can use the gentler training methods with great success.

Training a puppy aged 10 to 16 weeks (20 weeks at the most) is like working with a dry sponge in

a pool of water. The pup soaks up whatever you show him and constantly looks for more things to do and learn. At this early age, his body is not yet producing hormones, and therein lies the reason for such a high rate of success. Without hormones, he is focused on his owners and not particularly interested in investigating other places, dogs, people, etc. You are his leader: his provider of food, water, shelter and security. He latches onto you and wants to stay close. He will usually follow you from room to room, will not let you out of his sight when you are outdoors with

Puppies learn by watching their dam. Before your pup arrived at your home, he spent eight weeks observing his mother's manners and habits.

THE HAND THAT FEEDS

To a dog's way of thinking, your hands are like his mouth in terms of a defence mechanism. If you squeeze him too tightly, he might just bite you because that would be his normal response. This is not aggressive biting and, although all biting should be discouraged, you need the discipline in learning how to handle your dog.

him and will respond in like manner to the people and animals you encounter. If you greet a friend warmly, he will be happy to greet the person as well. If, however, you are hesitant or anxious about the approach of a stranger, he will respond accordingly.

HONOUR AND OBEY

Dogs are the most honourable animals in existence. They consider another species (humans) as their own. They interface with you. You are their leader. Puppies perceive children to be on their level; their actions around small children are different from their behaviour around their adult masters.

Once the puppy begins to produce hormones, his natural curiosity emerges and he begins to investigate the world around him. It is at this time when you may notice that the untrained dog begins to wander away from you and even ignore your commands to stay close. When this behaviour becomes a problem, you have two choices: get rid of the dog or train him. It is strongly urged that you choose the latter option.

You usually will be able to find obedience classes within a reasonable distance from your home, but you can also do a lot to train your dog yourself. Sometimes there are classes available, but the tuition is too costly. Whatever the circumstances, the solution to training your dog without obedience classes lies within the pages of this book.

This chapter is devoted to helping you train your Schnauzer at home. If the recommended procedures are followed faithfully, you may expect positive results that will prove rewarding both to you and your dog.

Whether your new charge is a puppy or a mature adult, the methods of teaching and the techniques we use in training basic behaviours are the same. After all, no dog, whether puppy or adult, likes harsh or inhumane methods. All creatures, however, respond favourably to gentle

CANINE DEVELOPMENT SCHEDULE

It is important to understand how and at what age a puppy develops into adulthood. If you are a puppy owner, consult the following Canine Development Schedule to determine the stage of development your puppy is currently experiencing. This knowledge will help you as you work with the puppy in the weeks and months ahead.

Period	Age	Characteristics
FIRST TO THIRD	BIRTH TO SEVEN WEEKS	Puppy needs food, sleep and warmth, and responds to simple and gentle touching. Needs mother for security and disciplining. Needs littermates for learning and interacting with other dogs. Pup learns to function within a pack and learns pack order of dominance. Begin socialising with adults and children for short periods. Begins to become aware of its environment.
FOURTH	EIGHT TO TWELVE WEEKS	Brain is fully developed. Needs socialising with outside world. Remove from mother and littermates. Needs to change from canine pack to human pack. Human dominance necessary. Fear period occurs between 8 and 12 weeks. Avoid fright and pain.
FIFTH	THIRTEEN TO SIXTEEN WEEKS	Training and formal obedience should begin. Less association with other dogs, more with people, places, situations. Period will pass easily if you remember this is pup's change-to-adolescence time. Be firm and fair. Flight instinct prominent. Permissiveness and over-disciplining can do permanent damage. Praise for good behaviour.
JUVENILE	FOUR TO EIGHT MONTHS	Another fear period about 7 to 8 months of age. It passes quickly, but be cautious of fright and pain. Sexual maturity reached. Dominant traits established. Dog should understand sit, down, come and stay by now.

NOTE: THESE ARE APPROXIMATE TIME FRAMES. ALLOW FOR INDIVIDUAL DIFFERENCES IN PUPPIES.

motivational methods and sincere praise and encouragement. Now let us get started.

TOILET TRAINING

You can train a puppy to relieve himself wherever you choose, but this must be somewhere suitable. You should bear in mind from the outset that when your puppy is old enough to go out in public places, any canine deposits must be removed at once. You will always have to carry with you a small plastic bag or 'poop-scoop.'

Outdoor training includes such surfaces as grass, soil and cement. Indoor training usually means training your dog to newspaper. When deciding on the surface and location that you will want your Schnauzer to use, be sure it is going to be permanent. Training your dog to grass and then changing your mind a few months later is extremely difficult for both dog and owner.

Next, choose the command you will use each and every time you want your puppy to void. 'Hurry up' and 'Toilet' are examples of commands commonly used by dog owners. The Schnauzer is a breed that takes very well to being trained to eliminate on command when started as a young pup. Get in the habit of giving the puppy your chosen relief command before you take him out. That way, when he becomes an adult, you will be

FEAR AGGRESSION
Pups who are subjected to physical abuse during training commonly end up with behavioural problems as adults. One common result of abuse is fear aggression, in which a dog will lash out, bare his teeth, snarl and finally bite someone by whom he feels threatened. For example, your daughter may be playing with the dog one afternoon. As they play hide-and-seek, she backs the dog into a corner and, as she attempts to tease him playfully, he bites her hand. Examine the cause of this behaviour. Did your daughter ever hit the dog? Did someone who resembles your daughter hit or scream at the dog?

Fortunately, fear aggression is relatively easy to correct. Have your daughter engage in only positive activities with the dog, such as feeding, petting and walking. She should not give any corrections or negative feedback. If the dog still growls or cowers away from her, allow someone else to accompany them. After approximately one week, the dog should feel that he can rely on her for many positive things, and he will also be prevented from reacting fearfully towards anyone who might resemble her.

able to determine if he wants to go out when you ask him. A confirmation will be signs of interest, wagging his tail,

SAFETY FIRST

While it may seem that the most important things to your dog are eating, sleeping and chewing the upholstery on your furniture, his first concern is actually safety. The domesticated dogs we keep as companions have the same pack instinct as their ancestors who ran free thousands of years ago. Because of this pack instinct, your dog wants to know that he and his pack are not in danger of being harmed, and that his pack has a strong, capable leader. You must establish yourself as the leader early on in your relationship. That way your dog will trust that you will take care of him and the pack, and he will accept your commands without question.

watching you intently, going to the door, etc.

PUPPY'S NEEDS

Puppy needs to relieve himself after play periods, after each meal, after he has been sleeping and at any time he indicates that he is looking for a place to urinate or defecate. The urinary and intestinal tract muscles of very young puppies are not fully developed. Therefore, like human babies, puppies need to relieve themselves frequently.

Take your puppy out often—every hour for an eight-week-old, for example—and always immedi-ately after sleeping and eating. The older the puppy, the less often he will need to relieve himself. Finally, as a mature healthy adult, he will require only three to five relief trips per day.

HOUSING

Since the types of housing and control you provide for your puppy have a direct relationship on the success of house-training, we consider the various aspects of both before we begin training.

Taking a new puppy home and turning him loose in your house can be compared to turning a child loose in a sports arena and telling the child that the place is all his! The sheer enormity of the place would be too much for him to handle. Instead, offer the puppy clearly defined areas where he can play, sleep, eat and live. A room of the house where the family gathers is the most obvious choice. Puppies are social animals and need to feel a part of the pack

Puppies need a leader to follow or else they will stray from the course.

KEY TO SUCCESS

Success that comes by luck is usually short-lived. Success that comes by well-thought-out proven methods is often more easily achieved and permanent. This is the Success Method. It is designed to give you, the puppy owner, a simple yet proven way to help your puppy develop clean living habits and a feeling of security in his new environment.

providing safety and security for both puppy and owner.

Within the designated room, there should be a smaller area that the puppy can call his own. An alcove, a wire or fibreglass dog crate or a fenced (not boarded!) corner from which he can view the activities of his new family will be fine. The size of the area or crate is the key factor here. The area must be large enough so that the puppy can lie down and stretch out, as well as stand up, without rubbing his head on the top. At the same time, it must be small enough so that he cannot relieve himself at one end and sleep at the other without coming into contact with his droppings before he is fully trained to relieve himself outside. Dogs are, by nature, clean animals and will not remain close to their relief areas unless forced to do so. In those cases, they then become dirty dogs and usually remain that way for life.

The dog's designated area should contain clean bedding and a toy. Water must always be available, in a non-spill container.

CONTROL

By control, we mean helping the puppy to create a lifestyle pattern that will be compatible to that of his human pack (YOU!). Just as we guide little children to learn our way of life, we must show the

right from the start. Hearing your voice, watching you while you are doing things and smelling you nearby are all positive reinforcers that he is now a member of your pack. Usually a family room, the kitchen or a nearby adjoining breakfast area is ideal for puppy when it is time to play, eat, sleep, exercise and even entertain himself.

Your puppy should always sleep in his crate. He should also learn that, during times of household confusion and excessive human activity, such as at breakfast when family members are preparing for the day, he can play by himself in relative safety and comfort in his designated area. Each time you leave the puppy alone, he should understand exactly where he is to stay.

Puppies are chewers. They cannot tell the difference between lamp cords, television wires, shoes, table legs, etc. Chewing into a television wire, for example, can be fatal to the puppy, while a shorted wire can start a fire in the house. If the puppy chews on the arm of the chair when he is alone, you will

THE SUCCESS METHOD

6 Steps to Successful Crate Training

1 Tell the puppy 'Crate time!' and place him in the crate with a small treat (a piece of cheese or half of a biscuit). Let him stay in the crate for five minutes while you are in the same room. Then release him and praise lavishly. Never release him when he is fussing. Wait until he is quiet before you let him out.

2 Repeat Step 1 several times a day.

3 The next day, place the puppy in the crate as before. Let him stay there for ten minutes. Do this several times.

4 Continue building time in five-minute increments until the puppy stays in his crate for 30 minutes with you in the room. Always take him to his relief area after prolonged periods in his crate.

5 Now go back to Step 1 and let the puppy stay in his crate for five minutes, this time while you are out of the room.

6 Once again, build crate time in five-minute increments with you out of the room. When the puppy will stay willingly in his crate (he may even fall asleep!) for 30 minutes with you out of the room, he will be ready to stay in it for several hours at a time.

probably discipline him angrily when you arrive at home. Thus, he makes the association that your coming home means he is going to be punished. (He will not remember chewing the chair and is incapable of making the associ-

HOUSE-TRAINING TIP

Most of all, be consistent. Always take your dog to the same location, always use the same command and always have the dog on lead when he is in his relief area, unless a fenced-in garden is available.

By following the Success Method, your puppy will be completely house-trained by the time his muscle and brain development reach maturity. Keep in mind that small breeds usually mature faster than large breeds, but all puppies should be trained by six months of age.

ation of the discipline with his naughty deed.) Accustoming the pup to his designated area not only keeps him safe but also avoids his engaging in destructive behaviours when you are not around.

Times of excitement, such as special occasions, family parties, etc., can be fun for the puppy, provided that he can view the activities from the security of his designated area. He is not underfoot and he is not being fed all sorts of titbits that will probably cause him stomach distress, yet he still feels a part of the fun.

SCHEDULE

A puppy should be taken to his relief area each time he is released from his designated area, after meals, after a play session and when he first awakens in the morning (at age eight weeks, this can mean 5 a.m.!). The puppy will indicate that he's ready 'to go' by circling or sniffing busily—do not misinterpret these signs. For a puppy less than ten weeks of age, a routine of taking him out every hour is necessary. As the puppy grows, he will be able to wait for longer periods of time.

Keep trips to his relief area short. Stay no more than five or six minutes and then return to the house. If he goes during that time, praise him lavishly and take him indoors immediately. If he does not, but he has an accident when you go back indoors, pick him up immediately, say 'No! No!' and return to his relief area. Wait a few minutes, then return to the house again. Never hit a puppy or rub his face in urine or excrement when he has had an accident!

Once indoors, put the puppy in his crate until you have had time to clean up his accident. Then, release him to the family area and watch him more closely than before. Chances are, his accident was a result of your not picking up his signal or waiting too long before offering him the opportunity to relieve himself. Never hold a grudge against the puppy for accidents.

Let the puppy learn that going outdoors means it is time to relieve himself, not to play. Once trained, he will be able to play indoors and out and still differentiate between the times for play versus the times for relief.

Help him develop regular hours for naps, being alone, playing by himself and just resting, all in his crate. Encourage him to entertain himself while you are busy with your activities. Let him learn that having you near is comforting, but it is not your main purpose in life to provide him with undivided attention.

Each time you put your puppy in his own area, use the same command, whatever suits best.

Soon he will run to his crate or special area when he hears you say those words.

Crate training provides safety for you, the puppy and the home. It also provides the puppy with a feeling of security, and that helps the puppy achieve self-confidence and clean habits. Remember that

HOW MANY TIMES A DAY?

AGE	RELIEF TRIPS
To 14 weeks	10
14–22 weeks	8
22–32 weeks	6
Adulthood	4
(dog stops growing)	

These are estimates, of course, but they are a guide to the MINIMUM opportunities a dog should have each day to relieve himself.

one of the primary ingredients in house-training your puppy is control. Regardless of your lifestyle, there will always be occasions when you will need to have a place where your dog can stay and be happy and safe. Crate training is the answer for now and in the future.

In conclusion, a few key elements are really all you need for a successful house-training method—consistency, frequency, praise, control and supervision. By following these procedures with a normal, healthy puppy, you and the puppy will soon be past the stage of 'accidents' and ready to move on to a clean and rewarding life together.

ROLES OF DISCIPLINE, REWARD AND PUNISHMENT

Discipline, training one to act in accordance with rules, brings order to life. It is as simple as that. Without discipline, particularly in a group society, chaos will reign supreme and the group will eventually perish. Humans and canines are social animals and need some form of discipline in order to function effectively. They must procure food, protect their home base and their young and reproduce to keep their species going. If there were no discipline in the lives of social animals, they would eventually die from starvation and/or predation by other stronger animals.

In the case of domestic canines, discipline in their lives is needed in order for them to understand how their pack (you and other family members) functions and how they must act in order to survive.

A large humane society in an highly populated area recently surveyed dog owners regarding their satisfaction with their relationships with their dogs. People who had trained their dogs were 75% more satisfied with their pets than those who had never trained their dogs.

Dr Edward Thorndike, a psychologist, established *Thorndike's Theory of Learning*, which states that a behaviour that results in a pleasant event tends to be repeated. A behaviour that results in an unpleasant event tends not to be repeated. It is this theory upon which training methods are based today. For example, if you manipulate a dog to perform a specific behaviour and reward him for doing it, he is likely to do it again because he enjoyed the end result.

Occasionally, punishment, a penalty inflicted for an offence, is necessary. The best type of punishment often comes from an outside source. For example, a child is told not to touch the stove because he may get burned. He disobeys and touches the stove. In doing so, he receives a burn. From that time on, he respects the heat of the stove and avoids contact with it. Therefore, a behaviour that results in an unpleasant event tends not to be repeated.

A good example of a dog learning the hard way is the dog who chases the house cat. He is told many times to leave the cat alone, yet he persists in teasing the cat. Then, one day, the dog begins chasing the cat but the cat turns and swipes a claw across the dog's face, leaving the dog with a painful gash on his nose. The final result is that the dog stops chasing the cat. Again, a behaviour that results in an unpleasant event tends not to be repeated.

TRAINING EQUIPMENT

COLLAR AND LEAD
For a Schnauzer, the collar and lead that you use for training must be one with which you are easily able to work, not too heavy for the dog and perfectly safe.

TREATS
Have a bag of treats on hand; something nutritious and easy to swallow works best. Use a soft treat, a chunk of cheese or a piece of cooked chicken rather than a dry biscuit. By the time the dog has finished chewing a dry treat, he will forget why he is being rewarded in the first place!

Using food rewards will not teach a dog to beg at the table—

the only way to teach a dog to beg at the table is to give him food from the table. In training, rewarding the dog with a food treat will help him associate praise and the treats with learning new behaviours that obviously please his owner.

TRAINING BEGINS: ASK THE DOG A QUESTION
In order to teach your dog anything, you must first get his attention. After all, he cannot learn anything if he is looking away from you with his mind on something else.

To get your dog's attention, ask him 'School?', and immediately walk over to him and give him a treat as you tell him 'Good dog.' Wait a minute or two and

Your Schnauzer will learn to accept the collar and lead as part of his education. Although the pup may fuss the first time you put on his collar, with encouragement he will accept it in no time.

THINK BEFORE YOU BARK

Dogs are sensitive to their masters'
moods and emotions. Use your voice
wisely when communicating with your
dog. Never raise your voice at your
dog unless you are angry and trying to
correct him. 'Barking' at your dog can
become as meaningless as 'dogspeak' is
to you. Think before you bark!

repeat the routine, this time with
a treat in your hand as you
approach within a foot of the dog.
Do not go directly to him, but stop
about a foot short of him and hold
out the treat as you ask 'School?'
He will see you approaching with
a treat in your hand and most
likely begin walking toward you.
As you meet, give him the treat
and praise again.

The third time, ask the
question, have a treat in your
hand and walk only a short
distance toward the dog so that he
must walk almost all the way to
you. As he reaches you, give him
the treat and praise again.

By this time, the dog will
probably be getting the idea that if
he pays attention to you,
especially when you ask that
question, it will pay off in treats
and enjoyable activities for him.
In other words, he learns that
'school' means doing great things
with you that are fun and that
result in positive attention for
him.

Remember that the dog does
not understand your verbal
language; he only recognises
sounds. Your question translates
to a series of sounds for him, and
those sounds become the signal to
go to you and pay attention. The
dog learns that if he does this, he
will get to interact with you plus
receive treats and praise.

THE BASIC COMMANDS

TEACHING SIT

Now that you have the dog's
attention, attach his lead and hold
it in your left hand, and hold a
food treat in your right hand.
Place your food hand at the dog's
nose and let him lick the treat but
not take it from you. Say 'Sit' and
slowly raise your food hand from
in front of the dog's nose up over

his head so that he is looking at the ceiling. As he bends his head upward, he will have to bend his knees to maintain his balance. As he bends his knees, he will assume a sit position. At that point, release the food treat and praise lavishly with comments such as 'Good dog! Good sit!,' etc. Remember to always praise enthusiastically, because dogs relish verbal praise from their owners and feel so proud of themselves whenever they accomplish a behaviour.

You will not use food forever in getting the dog to obey your commands. Food is only used to teach new behaviours and, once the dog knows what you want when you give a specific command, you will wean him off the food treats but still maintain the verbal praise. After all, you will always have your voice with you, and there will be many times when you have no food rewards but expect the dog to obey.

The sit exercise is usually the easiest lesson to teach. Always begin and end training sessions with a command that your dog has mastered.

TEACHING DOWN

Teaching the down exercise is easy when you understand how the dog perceives the down position, and it is very difficult when you do not. Dogs perceive the down position as a submissive one; therefore, teaching the down exercise by using a forceful method can sometimes make the dog develop such a fear of the down that he either runs away when you say 'Down' or he attempts to snap at the person who tries to force him down.

Have the dog sit close alongside your left leg, facing in the same direction as you are. Hold the lead in your left hand and a food treat in your right. Now place your left hand lightly on the top of the dog's shoulders where they meet above the spinal cord. Do not push down on the dog's shoulders; simply rest your

DOUBLE JEOPARDY

A dog in jeopardy never lies down. He stays alert on his feet because instinct tells him that he may have to run away or fight for his survival. Therefore, if a dog feels threatened or anxious, he will not lie down. Consequently, it is important to have the dog calm and relaxed as he learns the down exercise.

softly to the dog, saying things like, 'Do you want this treat? You can do this, good dog.' Your reassuring tone of voice will help calm the dog as he tries to follow the food hand in order to get the treat.

When the dog's elbows touch the floor, release the food and praise softly. Try to get the dog to maintain that down position for several seconds before you let him sit up again. The goal here is to get the dog to settle down and not feel threatened in the down position.

TEACHING STAY

It is easy to teach the dog to stay in either a sit or a down position. Again, we use food and praise during the teaching process as we help the dog to understand exactly what it is that we are expecting him to do.

To teach the sit/stay, start with the dog sitting on your left side as before and hold the lead in your left hand. Have a food treat in your right hand and place your food hand at the dog's nose. Say 'Stay' and step out on your right foot to stand directly in front of the dog, toe to toe, as he licks and nibbles the treat. Be sure to keep his head facing upward to maintain the sit position. Count to five and then swing around to stand next to the dog again with him on your left. As soon as you get back to the original position,

left hand there so you can guide the dog to lie down close to your left leg rather than to swing away from your side when he drops.

Now place the food hand at the dog's nose, say 'Down' very softly (almost a whisper), and slowly lower the food hand to the dog's front feet. When the food hand reaches the floor, begin moving it forward along the floor in front of the dog. Keep talking

release the food and praise lavishly.

To teach the down/stay, do the down as previously described. As soon as the dog lies down, say 'Stay' and step out on your right foot just as you did in the sit/stay. Count to five and then return to stand beside the dog with him on your left side. Release the treat and praise as always.

Within a week or ten days, you can begin to add a bit of distance between you and your dog when you leave him. When you do, use your left hand open with the palm facing the dog as a stay signal, much the same as the hand signal a constable uses to stop traffic at a junction. Hold the food treat in your right hand as before, but this time the food will not be touching the dog's nose. He

will watch the food hand and quickly learn that he is going to get that treat as soon as you return to his side.

When you can stand 1 metre away from your dog for 30 seconds, you can then begin building time and distance in both stays. Eventually, the dog can be expected to remain in the stay position for prolonged periods of time until you return to him or call him to you. Always praise lavishly when he stays.

TEACHING COME
Probably one of the hardest and most important commands to ensure that your Schnauzer responds to absolutely reliably is 'come.' This is especially true when there is a squirrel or other small, fast, scurrying-type animal

Teaching stay in either the down or sit position is a natural extension of those exercises. The stay will be useful under many circum-stances.

SCHNAUZER

within the Schnauzer's eyesight. The Schnauzer's inherited ratting instinct is extremely strong in some individuals, thus 'running interference' in your lesson plans. If you make teaching 'come' an exciting experience, you should never have a student that does not love the game or that fails to come when called. The secret, it seems, is never to teach the word 'come.'

At times when an owner most wants his dog to come when called, the owner is likely to be upset or anxious and he allows these feelings to come through in the tone of his voice when he calls his dog. Hearing that desperation in his owner's voice, the dog fears the results of going to him and therefore either disobeys outright or runs in the opposite direction. The secret, therefore, is to teach the dog a game and, when you want him to come to you, simply play the game. It is practically a no-fail solution!

To begin, have several members of your family take a few food treats and each go into a different room in the house. Everyone takes turns calling the dog, and each person should celebrate the dog's finding him with a treat and lots of happy praise. When a person calls the dog, he is actually inviting the dog to find him and to get a treat as a reward for 'winning.'

A few turns of the 'Where are you?' game and the dog will understand that everyone is playing the game and that each person has a big celebration awaiting the dog's success at locating him or her. Once the dog learns to love the game, simply calling out 'Where are you?' will bring him running from wherever he is when he hears that all-important question.

The come command is recognised as one of the most important things to teach a dog,

'COME' . . . BACK

Never call your dog to come to you for a correction or scold him when he reaches you. That is the quickest way to turn a 'Come' command into 'Go away fast!' Dogs think only in the present tense, and your dog will connect the scolding with coming to you, not with the misbehaviour of a few moments earlier.

but there are trainers who work with thousands of dogs and never teach the actual word 'come.' Yet these dogs will race to respond to a person who uses the dog's name followed by 'Where are you?' For example, a woman has a 12-year-old companion dog who went blind, but who never fails to locate her owner when asked, 'Where are you?'

Children, in particular, love to play this game with their dogs. Children can hide in smaller places like a shower or bath, behind a bed or under a table. The dog needs to work a little bit harder to find these hiding places, but, when he does, he loves to celebrate with a treat and a tussle with a favourite youngster.

Never underestimate the power of food! Most dogs will respond with greater interest if there is a tasty titbit at stake.

TEACHING HEEL

Heeling means that the dog walks beside the owner without pulling. It takes time and patience on the owner's part to succeed at teaching the dog that he (the owner) will not proceed unless the dog is walking calmly beside him. Neither pulling out ahead on the lead nor lagging behind is acceptable.

Begin by holding the lead in your left hand as the dog sits beside your left leg. Move the loop end of the lead to your right hand, but keep your left hand short on the lead so that it keeps the dog in close next to you.

Say 'Heel' and step forward on your left foot. Keep the dog close to you and take three steps. Stop and have the dog sit next to you in what we now call the 'heel position.' Praise verbally, but do not touch the dog. Hesitate a moment and begin again with 'Heel,' taking three steps and stopping, at which point the dog is told to sit again.

Your goal here is to have the dog walk those three steps without pulling on the lead. Once he will walk calmly beside you for three steps without pulling, increase the number of steps you take to five. When he will walk politely beside you while you take five steps, you can increase the length of your walk to ten steps. Keep increasing the length of your stroll until the dog will walk quietly beside you without pulling as long as you want him to heel. When you stop heeling, indicate to the dog that the exercise is over by verbally praising as you pet him and say 'OK, good dog.' The 'OK' is used as a release word, meaning that the exercise is finished and the dog is free to relax.

TUG OF WALK?

If you begin teaching the heel by taking long walks and letting the dog pull you along, he misinterprets this action as an acceptable form of taking a walk. When you pull back on the lead to counteract his pulling, he reads that tug as a signal to pull even harder!

WEANING OFF FOOD IN TRAINING

Food is used in training new behaviours. Once the dog understands what behaviour goes with a specific command, it is time to start weaning him off the food treats. At first, give a treat after each exercise. Then, start to give a treat only after every other exercise. Mix up the times when you offer a food reward and the times when you only offer praise so that the dog will never know when he is going to receive both food and praise and when he is going to receive only praise. This is called a variable ratio reward system. It proves successful because there is always the chance that the owner will produce a treat, so the dog never stops trying for that reward. No matter what, ALWAYS give verbal praise.

If you are dealing with a dog who insists on pulling you around, simply 'put on your brakes' and stand your ground until the dog realises that the two of you are not going anywhere until he is beside you and moving at your pace, not his. It may take some time just standing there to convince the dog that you are the leader and that you will be the one to decide on the direction and speed of your travel.

Each time the dog looks up at you or slows down to give a slack lead between the two of you, quietly praise him and say, 'Good heel. Good dog.' Eventually, the dog will begin to respond and within a few days he will be walking politely beside you without pulling on the lead. At first, the training sessions should be kept short and very positive; soon the dog will be able to walk nicely with you for increasingly longer distances. Remember also to give the dog free time and the opportunity to run and play when you have finished heel practice.

OBEDIENCE CLASSES
It is a good idea to enrol in an obedience class if one is available in your area. If yours is a show dog, ringcraft classes would be more appropriate. Many areas have dog clubs that offer basic obedience training as well as preparatory classes for obedience competition. There are also local dog trainers who offer similar classes.

Heeling requires that the Schnauzer walk at your side at your speed. Once the dog understands this concept, he will be a pleasure to walk. You can be certain that being pulled down the lane by an unruly Schnauzer is no fun.

At obedience shows, dogs can earn titles at various levels of competition. The beginning levels of obedience competition include basic behaviours such as sit, down, heel, etc. The more advanced levels of competition include jumping, retrieving, scent discrimination and signal work. The advanced levels require a dog and owner to put a lot of time and effort into their training. The titles that can be earned at these levels of competition are very prestigious.

OTHER ACTIVITIES FOR LIFE
The Schnauzer is, mentally and physically, probably one of the most versatile breeds of dog. Most Schnauzers are very well suited to

HEELING WELL
Teach your dog to heel in an enclosed area. Once you think the dog will obey reliably and you want to attempt advanced obedience exercises such as off-lead heeling, test him in a fenced-in area so he cannot run away.

Although not one of the Schnauzer's bred-for abilities, lure coursing is not beyond the scope or stride of the breed.

Tracking trials are popular in the US, where Schnauzers apply their sensational noses to find articles laid on a track.

The breed certainly does hold its own in formal competition when trained by a good owner-trainer. Probably the reason that they are not one of the more popular canine competitors is the high maintenance required for their coats, making year-round competition doubly time-consuming. The handler needs both time for training and time for grooming.

Nevertheless, Schnauzers participate with devotees of our breed in many formal and informal dog sports, such as obedience, tracking, agility, flyball and, most recently, herding and lure coursing, to name a few. With its strongly muscled, square, compact body, combined with an extraordinary degree of canine intelligence, this is truly a most versatile companion animal.

Some Schnauzer owners also have the opportunity to participate in the classic German training/competition programme known as Schutzhund, although this is more commonly pursued by the Schnauzer's 'Giant' cousin. Although originally bred as terriers, Schnauzers make excellent watchdogs, and their high degree of intelligence recommends them for these specialised tests.

Schutzhund originated as a test to determine the best quality working/protection dogs to be used for breeding stock. Breeders

participate in most any dog sport or type of work that a person can dream up. The Schnauzer's amazing attention to detail, very strong, determined mind and never-ending curiosity have made the breed successful as hearing dogs for the deaf, assistance dogs for the handicapped, pet therapists in critical-care hospitals and nursing homes, police workers, search and rescue (SAR) dogs, melanoma cancer detection dogs and even as retrievers of bird in the field. You name it and a Schnauzer has done it...or is doing it.

on the Continent and in the US continue to use it as a way to evaluate working ability and temperament. There are three levels in Schutzhund trials: SchH I, SchH II and SchH III, with each level being progressively more difficult to complete successfully. Each level consists of training, obedience and protection phases. Training for Schutzhund is intense and must be practised consistently to keep the dog keen. The experience of Schutzhund training is very rewarding for dog and owner, and the Schnauzer is well suited for this type of training.

TRAINING TIP
If you are walking your dog and he suddenly stops and looks straight into your eyes, ignore him. Pull the leash and lead him into the direction you want to walk.

Schnauzers naturally adapt to the demands of herding trials, as this talented California dog illustrates with great panache.

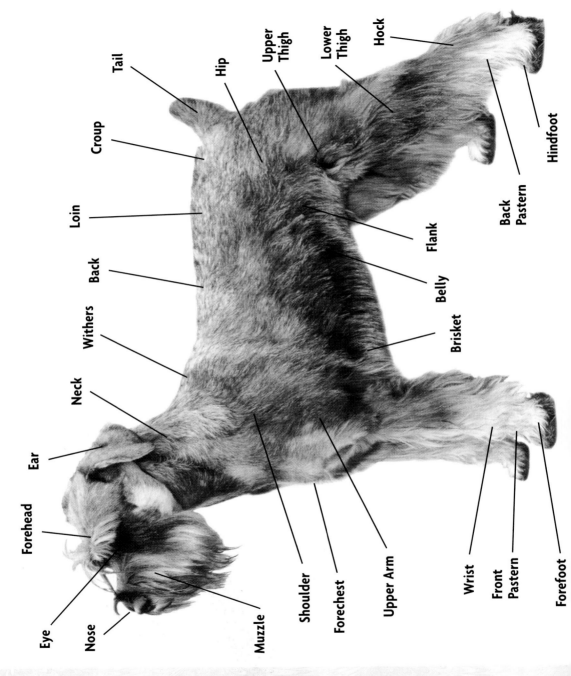

Forehead

Ear

Neck

Withers

Back

Loin

Croup

Tail

Hip

Upper Thigh

Lower Thigh

Hock

Back Pastern

Hindfoot

Flank

Belly

Brisket

Eye

Nose

Muzzle

Shoulder

Forechest

Upper Arm

Wrist

Front Pastern

Forefoot

PHYSICAL STRUCTURE OF THE SCHNAUZER

Health Care of Your
SCHNAUZER

Dogs suffer from many of the same physical illnesses as people. They might even share many of the same psychological problems. Since people usually know more about human diseases than canine maladies, many of the terms used in this chapter will be familiar but not necessarily those used by veterinary surgeons. We will use the term *x-ray*, instead of the more acceptable term *radiograph*. We will also use the familiar term *symptoms* even though dogs don't have symptoms, which are verbal descriptions of the patient's feelings; dogs have *clinical signs*. Since dogs can't speak, we have to look for clinical signs...but we still use the term *symptoms* in this book.

As a general rule, medicine is *practised*. That term is not arbitrary. Medicine is a constantly changing art as we learn more and more about genetics, electronic aids (like CAT scans) and daily laboratory advances. There are many dog maladies, like canine hip dysplasia, which are not universally treated in the same manner. Some veterinary surgeons opt for surgery more often than others do.

SELECTING A VETERINARY SURGEON

Your selection of a veterinary surgeon should not be based soley upon personality (as most are) but also upon his abilities and his convenience to your home. You want a vet who is close because you might have emergencies or need to make multiple visits for treatments. You want a vet who has services that you might require such as tattooing and grooming, as well as sophisticated pet supplies and a good reputation for ability and responsiveness. There is nothing more frustrating than having to wait a day or more to get a response from your veterinary surgeon.

All veterinary surgeons are licenced and their diplomas and/or certificates should be displayed in their waiting rooms. There are, however, many veterinary specialities that usually require further studies and internships. There are specialists in heart problems (veterinary cardiologists), skin problems (veterinary dermatologists), teeth and gum problems (veterinary dentists), eye problems (veterinary ophthalmologists) and x-rays (veterinary radiologists), as

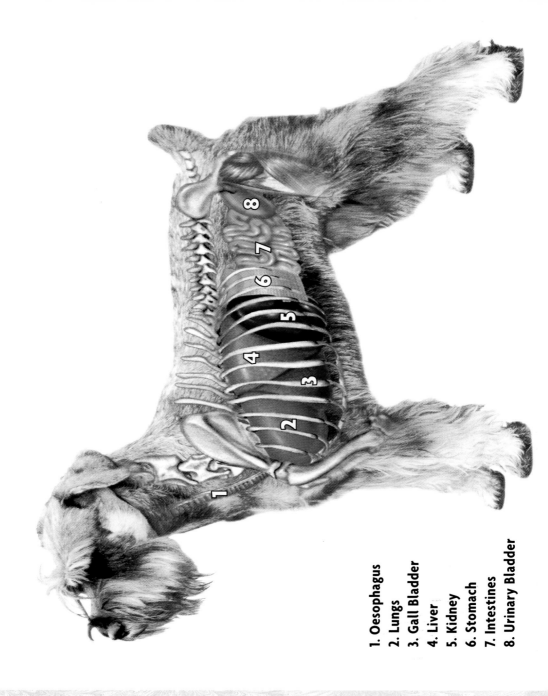

1. Oesophagus
2. Lungs
3. Gall Bladder
4. Liver
5. Kidney
6. Stomach
7. Intestines
8. Urinary Bladder

INTERNAL ORGANS OF THE SCHNAUZER

well as vets who have specialities in bones, muscles or other organs. Most veterinary surgeons do routine surgery such as neutering, stitching up wounds and docking tails for those breeds in which such is required for show purposes.

When the problem affecting your dog is serious, it is not unusual or impudent to get another medical opinion, although in Britain you are obliged to advise the vets concerned about this. You might also want to compare costs among several veterinary surgeons. Sophisticated health care and veterinary services can be very costly. It is not infrequent that important decisions are based upon financial considerations.

PREVENTATIVE MEDICINE

It is much easier, less costly and more effective to practise preventative medicine than to fight bouts of illness and disease. Properly bred puppies come from parents who were selected based upon their genetic disease profiles. Their mothers should have been vaccinated, free of all internal and external parasites and properly nourished. The dam can pass on disease resistance to her puppies, which can last for eight to ten weeks, but she can also pass on parasites and many infections. For these reasons, a visit to the veterinary surgeon who cared for the dam is recommended.

Breakdown of Veterinary Income by Category

2%	Dentistry
4%	Radiology
12%	Surgery
15%	Vaccinations
19%	Laboratory
23%	Examinations
25%	Medicines

VACCINATION SCHEDULING

Most vaccinations are given by injection and should only be done by a veterinary surgeon. Both he and you should keep records of the date of the injection, the identification of the vaccine and the amount given. Some vets give a first vaccination at eight weeks, but most dog breeders prefer the course not to commence until about ten weeks to avoid negating any antibodies passed on by the dam. The vaccination scheduling is usually based on a 15-day cycle. You must take your vet's advice regarding when to vaccinate, as this may differ according to the vaccine used. Most vaccinations immunize your puppy against viruses.

The usual vaccines contain immunizing doses of several different viruses such as distemper, parvovirus, parainfluenza and

A typical American vet's income, categorised according to services performed. This survey dealt with small-animal (pets) practices.

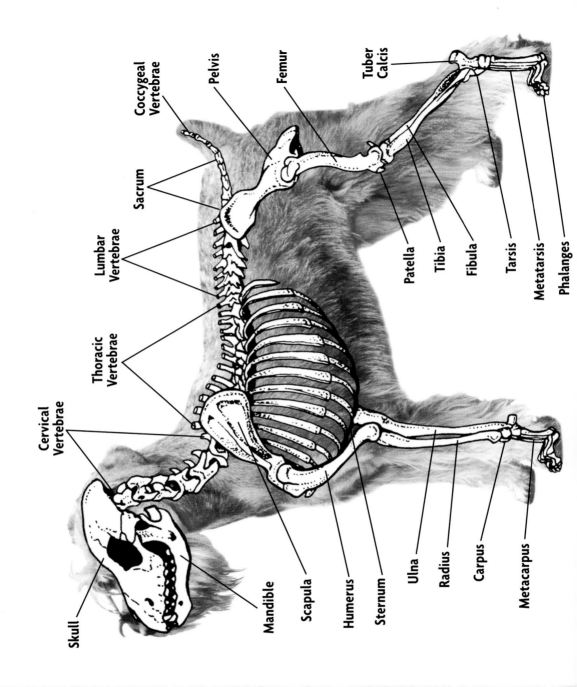

Coccygeal Vertebrae

Pelvis

Femur

Tuber Calcis

Sacrum

Lumbar Vertebrae

Patella

Tibia

Fibula

Tarsis

Metatarsis

Phalanges

Thoracic Vertebrae

Cervical Vertebrae

Skull

Mandible

Scapula

Humerus

Sternum

Ulna

Radius

Carpus

Metacarpus

SKELETAL STRUCTURE OF THE SCHNAUZER

hepatitis, although some veterinary surgeons recommend separate vaccines for each disease. There are other vaccines available when the puppy is at risk. You should rely upon professional advice. This is especially true for the booster-shot programme. Most vaccination programmes require a booster when the puppy is a year old and once a year thereafter. In some cases, circumstances may require more or less frequent immunizations. Kennel cough, more formally known as tracheo-bronchitis, is treated with a vaccine that is sprayed into the dog's nostrils. Kennel cough is usually included in routine vaccination, but this is often not so effective as for other major diseases.

WEANING TO FIVE MONTHS OLD

Puppies should be weaned by the time they are about two months old. A puppy that remains for at least eight weeks with its mother and littermates usually adapts better to other dogs and people later in life. Some new owners have their puppies examined by veterinary surgeons immediately, which is a good idea. Vaccination programmes usually begin when the puppy is very young.

The puppy will have its teeth examined, and have its skeletal

HEALTH AND VACCINATION SCHEDULE

AGE IN WEEKS:	6TH	8TH	10TH	12TH	14TH	16TH	20-24TH	52ND
Worm Control	✔	✔	✔	✔	✔	✔	✔	
Neutering								✔
Heartworm		✔		✔		✔	✔	
Parvovirus	✔		✔		✔		✔	✔
Distemper		✔		✔		✔		✔
Hepatitis		✔		✔		✔		✔
Leptospirosis								✔
Parainfluenza	✔		✔		✔			✔
Dental Examination		✔					✔	✔
Complete Physical		✔					✔	✔
Coronavirus				✔			✔	✔
Kennel Cough	✔							
Hip Dysplasia								✔
Rabies							✔	

Vaccinations are not instantly effective. It takes about two weeks for the dog's immune system to develop antibodies. Most vaccinations require annual booster shots. Your veterinary surgeon should guide you in this regard.

DO YOU KNOW ABOUT HIP DYSPLASIA?

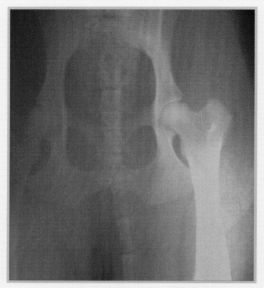

X-ray of a dog with 'Good' hips.

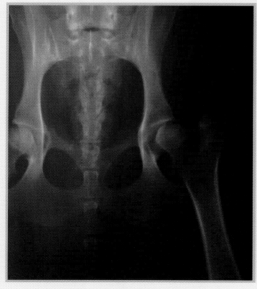

X-ray of a dog with 'Moderate' dysplastic hips.

Hip dysplasia is a fairly common condition found in pure-bred dogs. When a dog has hip dysplasia, its hind leg has an incorrectly formed hip joint. By constant use of the hip joint, it becomes more and more loose, wears abnormally and may become arthritic.

Hip dysplasia can only be confirmed with an x-ray, but certain symptoms may indicate a problem. Your dog may have a hip dysplasia problem if it walks in a peculiar manner, hops instead of smoothly runs, uses its hind legs in unison (to keep the pressure off the weak joint), has trouble getting up from a prone position or always sits with both legs together on one side of its body.

As the dog matures, it may adapt well to life with a bad hip, but in a few years the arthritis develops and many dogs with hip dysplasia become cripples.

Hip dysplasia is considered an inherited disease and only can be diagnosed definitively when the dog is two years old. Some experts claim that a special diet might help your puppy outgrow the bad hip, but the usual treatments are surgical. The removal of the pectineus muscle, the removal of the round part of the femur, reconstructing the pelvis and replacing the hip with an artificial one are all surgical interventions that are expensive, but they are usually very successful. Follow the advice of your veterinary surgeon.

DISEASE REFERENCE CHART

	What is it?	What causes it?	Symptoms
Leptospirosis	Severe disease that affects the internal organs; can be spread to people.	A bacterium, which is often carried by rodents, that enters through mucous membranes and spreads quickly throughout the body.	Range from fever, vomiting and loss of appetite in less severe cases to shock, irreversible kidney damage and possibly death in most severe cases.
Rabies	Potentially deadly virus that infects warm-blooded mammals. Not seen in United Kingdom.	Bite from a carrier of the virus, mainly wild animals.	1st stage: dog exhibits change in behaviour, fear. 2nd stage: dog's behaviour becomes more aggressive. 3rd stage: loss of coordination, trouble with bodily functions.
Parvovirus	Highly contagious virus, potentially deadly.	Ingestion of the virus, which is usually spread through the faeces of infected dogs.	Most common: severe diarrhoea. Also vomiting, fatigue, lack of appetite.
Kennel cough	Contagious respiratory infection.	Combination of types of bacteria and virus. Most common: *Bordetella bronchiseptica* bacteria and parainfluenza virus.	Chronic cough.
Distemper	Disease primarily affecting respiratory and nervous system.	Virus that is related to the human measles virus.	Mild symptoms such as fever, lack of appetite and mucous secretion progress to evidence of brain damage, 'hard pad.'
Hepatitis	Virus primarily affecting the liver.	Canine adenovirus type I (CAV-1). Enters system when dog breathes in particles.	Lesser symptoms include listlessness, diarrhoea, vomiting. More severe symptoms include 'blue-eye' (clumps of virus in eye).
Coronavirus	Virus resulting in digestive problems.	Virus is spread through infected dog's faeces.	Stomach upset evidenced by lack of appetite, vomiting, diarrhoea.

conformation and general health checked prior to certification by the veterinary surgeon. Puppies in certain breeds may have problems with their kneecaps, cataracts and other eye problems, heart murmurs or undescended testicles. They may also have personality problems, and your veterinary surgeon might have training in temperament evaluation.

FIVE TO TWELVE MONTHS OF AGE
Unless you intend to breed or show your dog, neutering the puppy at six months of age is recommended. Discuss this with your veterinary surgeon. Neutering has proven to be extremely beneficial to both male and female puppies. Besides eliminating the possibility of pregnancy, it inhibits (but does not prevent) breast cancer in bitches and prostate cancer in male dogs. Under no circumstances should a bitch be spayed prior to her first season.

Your veterinary surgeon should provide your puppy with a thorough dental evaluation at six months of age, ascertaining whether all the permanent teeth have erupted properly. An home dental care regimen should be initiated at six months, including brushing weekly and providing good dental devices (such as nylon bones). Regular dental care promotes healthy teeth, fresh breath and a longer life.

ONE YEAR AND OLDER
Once a year, your grown dog should visit the vet for an examination and vaccination boosters, if needed. Some vets recommend blood tests, a thyroid level check and a dental evaluation to accompany these annual visits. A thorough clinical evaluation by the vet can provide critical background information for your dog. Blood tests are often performed at one year of age, and dental examinations around the third or fourth birthday. In the long run, quality preventative care for your pet can save money, teeth and lives.

HEREDITARY DISORDERS IN THE SCHNAUZER
By and large, the Schnauzer is an healthy, hardy breed of dog that enjoys a long lifespan, often to 17 or 18 years of age. This is impressive for any breed of dog, no matter the size. Owners (and potential owners) should be cautioned, however, of some problems that have occurred in the breed over which breeders and vets voice some concern. Breeders world-wide are constantly trying to keep genetic defects to a minimum.

Fortunately, Schnauzers are relatively free of most genetic problems that plague some of the other breeds. Hip dysplasia has been documented in some Schnauzers, though the problem is not as widespread as in most other working breeds, and severe dysplasia is rare. Hip dysplasia (HD) refers to the abnormal development of the hip in which the ball and socket fail to function properly. X-rays can determine whether the Schnauzer is affected by this disease, which is considered to be inherited. Therefore, breeders routinely screen their stock so that dysplastic animals are not included in their breeding programmes. Puppy buyers should discuss this with their breeders. X-ray results are only conclusive once the dog has reached two years of age.

Very few breeders have encountered thyroid, eye problems or epilepsy, but there have been a few cases reported. Hypothyroidism refers to low activity of the thyroid gland; affected dogs require a thyroid-stimulating hormone (TSH) response test in addition to the standard t4 thyroid test to diagnose the disorder.

Epilepsy, in its inherited or idiopathic form, occurs in a number of breeds. It affects the dog's neurological system, resulting in recurring seizures or

THE SAME ALLERGIES
Chances are that you and your dog will have the same allergies. Your allergies are readily recognisable and usually easily treated. Your dog's allergies may be masked.

rare!). For this reason, veterinary dermatology has developed into a speciality practised by many veterinary surgeons.

Since many skin problems have visual symptoms that are almost identical, it requires the skill of an experienced veterinary dermatologist to identify and cure many of the more severe skin disorders. Pet shops sell many treatments for skin problems, but most of the treatments are directed at the symptoms and not the underlying problem(s). If your dog is suffering from a skin disorder, you should seek profes-sional assistance as quickly as possible. As with all diseases, the earlier a problem is identified and treated, the more successful is the cure.

convulsions. Usually epilepsy can be identified when the dog is between six months and three years of age.

The one problem that causes most Schnauzers'early demise, besides the automobile, is one that has become alarmingly prevalent in many breeds of dog (as well as in humans)—cancer. Discuss the prevalence of cancer in the breeder's line before committing to purchasing a puppy. Cancer can develop in an animal at any age, but commonly at an older age. Breeders may have to research not just the granddam and grandsire of the litter, but perhaps go back as many as three or four generations.

SKIN PROBLEMS
Veterinary surgeons are consulted by dog owners for skin problems more than for any other group of diseases or maladies, and Schnauzers commonly suffer from minor skin problems. Dogs' skin is almost as sensitive as human skin, and both suffer from almost the same ailments (though the occurrence of acne in dogs is

HEREDITARY SKIN DISORDERS
Veterinary dermatologists are currently researching a number of skin disorders that are believed to have an hereditary basis. These inherited diseases are transmitted by both parents, who appear (phenotypically) normal but have a recessive gene for the disease, meaning that they carry, but are not affected by, the disease. These diseases pose serious problems to breeders because in some instances there are no methods of identifying carriers. Often the secondary diseases associated with these skin conditions are even more debilitating than the

MANY KINDS OF EARS

Not every dog's ears are the same. Ears that are open to the air are healthier than ears with poor air circulation. Sometimes a dog can have two differently shaped ears. You should not probe inside your dog's ears. Only clean that which is accessible with a soft cotton wipe.

your dog is bitten by a flea, tick or mite, he can only scratch it away or bite it. By the time the dog has been bitten, the parasite has done some of its damage. It may also have laid eggs, which will cause further problems in the near future. The itching from parasite bites is probably due to the saliva injected into the site when the parasite sucks the dog's blood.

skin disorders themselves, including cancers and respiratory problems.

Among the hereditary skin disorders, for which the mode of inheritance is known, are acrodermatitis, cutaneous asthenia (Ehlers-Danlos syndrome), sebaceous adenitis, cyclic hematopoiesis, dermatomyositis, IgA deficiency, colour dilution alopaecia and nodular dermatofibrosis. Some of these disorders are limited to one or two breeds, while others affect a large number of breeds. All inherited diseases must be diagnosed and treated by a veterinary specialist.

PARASITE BITES

Many of us are allergic to insect bites. The bites itch, erupt and may even become infected. Dogs have the same reaction to fleas, ticks and/or mites. When an insect lands on you, you have the chance to whisk it away with your hand. Unfortunately, when

AUTO-IMMUNE SKIN CONDITIONS

An auto-immune skin condition is commonly referred to as a condition in which a person (or dog) is 'allergic' to him- or

A SKUNKY PROBLEM

Have you noticed your dog dragging his rump along the floor? If so, it is likely that his anal sacs are impacted or possibly infected. The anal sacs are small pouches located on both sides of the anus under the skin and muscles. They are about the size and shape of a grape and contain a foul-smelling liquid. Their contents are usually emptied when the dog has a bowel movement but, if not emptied completely, they will impact, which will cause your dog much pain. Fortunately, your veterinary surgeon can tend to this problem easily by draining the sacs for the dog. Be aware that your dog might also empty his anal sacs in cases of extreme fright.

herself, while an allergy is usually an inflammatory reaction to an outside stimulus. Auto-immune diseases cause serious damage to the tissues that are involved.

The best known auto-immune disease is lupus, which affects people as well as dogs. The symptoms are variable and may affect the kidneys, bones, blood chemistry and skin. It can be fatal to both dogs and humans, though it is not thought to be transmissible. It is usually successfully treated with cortisone, prednisone or a similar corticosteroid, but extensive use of these drugs can have harmful side effects.

ACRAL LICK GRANULOMA

Many dogs have a very poorly understood syndrome called acral lick granuloma. The manifestation of the problem is the dog's tireless attack at a specific area of the body, frequently the legs or paws. The dog licks so intensively that he removes the hair and skin, leaving an ugly, large wound. Tiny protuberances, which are outgrowths of new capillaries, bead on the surface of the wound. Owners who notice their dogs' biting and chewing at their extremities should have the vet determine the cause. If lick granuloma is identified, although there is no absolute cure, corticosteroids are one common treatment.

AIRBORNE ALLERGIES

Just as humans have hay fever, rose fever and other fevers from which they suffer during the pollinating season, many dogs suffer from these same allergies. As when the pollen count is high, your dog might suffer, but don't expect him to sneeze and have a runny nose as a human would. Dogs react to pollen allergies the same way they react to fleas—they scratch and bite themselves. Dogs, like humans, can be tested for allergens. Discuss the testing with your veterinary dermatologist.

FOOD PROBLEMS

FOOD ALLERGIES

Food allergies are fairly common in the Schnauzer, so owners must be aware of the chances of their dogs' suffering from this nuisance of a problem. Dogs are allergic to many foods that are best-sellers and highly recommended by

Soundness and quality beget the same: These dogs represent three generations of international champion Schnauzers from Sweden.

breeders and veterinary surgeons. Changing the brand of food that you buy may not eliminate the problem if the element to which the dog is allergic is contained in the new brand.

Recognising a food allergy is difficult. Humans vomit or have rashes when they eat a food to which they are allergic. Dogs neither vomit nor (usually) develop rashes. They react in the same manner as they would to an airborne or flea allergy; they itch, scratch and bite, thus making the diagnosis extremely difficult. While pollen allergies and parasite bites are usually seasonal, food allergies are year-round problems.

FOOD INTOLERANCE
Food intolerance is the inability of the dog to completely digest certain foods. For instance, puppies that may have done very well on their mother's milk may not do well on cow's milk. The results of food intolerance may be evident in loose bowels, passing gas and stomach pains. These are the only obvious symptoms of food intolerance, which makes diagnosis difficult.

TREATING FOOD PROBLEMS
It is possible to handle food allergies and food intolerance yourself. Start by putting your dog on a diet that he has never had. Obviously, if the dog has never

KNOW WHEN TO POSTPONE A VACCINATION
While the visit to the vet is costly, it is never advisable to update a vaccination when visiting with a sick or pregnant dog. Vaccinations should be avoided for all elderly dogs. If your dog is showing the signs of any illness or any medical condition, no matter how serious or mild, including skin irritations, do not vaccinate. Likewise, a lame dog should never be vaccinated; any dog undergoing surgery or on any immunosuppressant drugs should not be vaccinated until fully recovered.

eaten this new food, he can't have been allergic or intolerant of it. Start with a single ingredient that is not in the dog's diet at the present time. Ingredients like chopped beef or chicken are common in dogs' diets, so try something more exotic like rabbit, pheasant or even just vegetables. Keep the dog on this diet (with no additives) for a month. If the symptoms of food allergy or intolerance disappear, it is quite likely that your dog has a food allergy.

Don't think that the single ingredient cured the problem. You still must find a suitable diet and

While exercising in your garden, your Schnauzer may develop a pollen allergy or some other airborne allergy. Also, be sure your lawns are not treated with harmful chemicals or fertilisers.

ascertain which ingredient in the old diet was objectionable. This is most easily done by adding ingredients to the new diet one at a time. Let the dog stay on the

FAT OR FICTION?

The myth that dogs need extra fat in their diets can be harmful. Should your vet recommend extra fat, use safflower oil instead of animal oils. Safflower oil has been shown to be less likely to cause allergic reactions.

modified diet for a month before you add another ingredient. Eventually, you will determine the ingredient that caused the adverse reaction.

An alternative method is to carefully study the ingredients in the diet to which your dog is allergic or intolerant. Identify the main ingredient in this diet and eliminate the main ingredient by buying a different food that does not have that ingredient. Keep experimenting until the symptoms disappear after one month on the new diet.

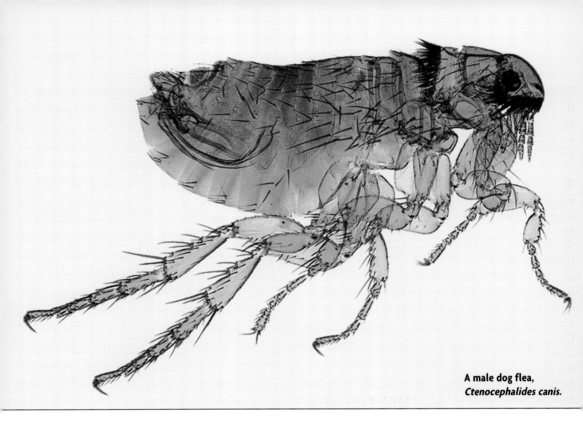

**A male dog flea,
*Ctenocephalides canis.***

EXTERNAL PARASITES

FLEAS
Of all the problems to which dogs are prone, none is more well known and frustrating than fleas. Flea infestation is relatively simple to cure but difficult to prevent. Parasites that are harboured inside the body are a bit more difficult to eradicate but they are easier to control.

To control flea infestation, you have to understand the flea's life cycle. Fleas are often thought of as a summertime problem, but centrally heated homes have changed the patterns and fleas can be found at any time of the year.

The most effective method of flea control is a two-stage approach: one stage to kill the adult fleas, and the other to control the development of pre-adult fleas. Unfortunately, no single active ingredient is effective against all stages of the life cycle.

LIFE CYCLE STAGES
During its life, a flea will pass through four life stages: egg, larva, pupa and adult. The adult stage is the most visible and irritating stage of the flea life cycle, and this is why the majority of flea-control products concentrate on this stage. The fact is that adult fleas account for only 1% of the total

flea population, and the other 99% exist in pre-adult stages, i.e. eggs, larvae and pupae. The pre-adult stages are barely visible to the naked eye.

THE LIFE CYCLE OF THE FLEA

Eggs are laid on the dog, usually in quantities of about 20 or 30, several times a day. The adult female flea must have a blood meal before each egg-laying session. When first laid, the eggs will cling to the dog's hair, as the eggs are still moist. However, they will quickly dry out and fall from the dog, especially if the dog moves around or scratches. Many eggs will fall off in the dog's favourite area or an area in which he spends a lot of time, such as his bed.

Once the eggs fall from the dog onto the carpet or furniture, they will hatch into larvae. This takes from one to ten days. Larvae are not particularly mobile and will usually travel only a few

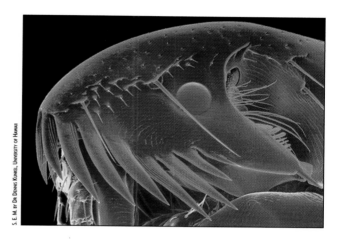

S.E.M. BY DR DENNIS KUNKEL, UNIVERSITY OF HAWAII

Magnified head of a dog flea, *Ctenocephalides canis*, colorized for effect.

inches from where they hatch. However, they do have a tendency to move away from light and heavy traffic—under furniture and behind doors are common places to find high quantities of flea larvae.

The flea larvae feed on dead organic matter, including adult flea faeces, until they are ready to change into adult fleas. Fleas will usually remain as larvae for around seven days. After this period, the larvae will pupate into protective pupae. While inside the pupae, the larvae will undergo metamorphosis and change into adult fleas. This can take as little time as a few days, but the adult fleas can remain inside the pupae waiting to hatch for up to two years. The pupae are signalled to hatch by certain stimuli, such as physical pressure—the pupae's being stepped on, heat from an animal's lying on the pupae or

FLEA KILLERS

Flea-killers are poisonous. You should not spray these toxic chemicals on areas of a dog's body that he licks, on his genitals or on his face. Flea killers taken internally are a better answer, but check with your vet in case internal therapy is not advised for your dog.

The dog flea is the most common parasite found on pet dogs.

S. E. M. BY DR DENNIS KUNKEL, UNIVERSITY OF HAWAII

increased carbon-dioxide levels and vibrations—indicating that a suitable host is available.

Once hatched, the adult flea must feed within a few days. Once the adult flea finds an host, it will not leave voluntarily. It only becomes dislodged by grooming or the host animal's scratching. The adult flea will remain on the host for the duration of its life unless forcibly removed.

Dwight R Kuhn's magnificent action photo, showing a flea jumping from a dog's back.

PHOTO BY DWIGHT R KUHN

TREATING THE ENVIRONMENT AND THE DOG

Treating fleas should be a two-pronged attack. First, the environment needs to be treated; this includes carpets and furniture, especially the dog's bedding and areas underneath furniture. The environment should be treated with an household spray containing an Insect Growth Regulator (IGR) and an insecticide to kill the adult fleas. Most IGRs are effective against eggs and larvae; they actually mimic the fleas' own hormones and stop the eggs and larvae from developing into adult fleas. There are currently no treatments available to attack the pupa stage of the life cycle, so the adult insecticide is used to kill the newly hatched adult fleas before they find an host. Most IGRs are active for many months, while adult insecticides are only active for a few days.

When treating with an household spray, it is a good idea to vacuum before applying the product. This stimulates as many pupae as possible to hatch into adult fleas. The vacuum cleaner should also be treated with an insecticide to prevent the eggs and larvae that have been hoovered into the vacuum bag from hatching.

The second stage of treatment is to apply an adult insecticide to

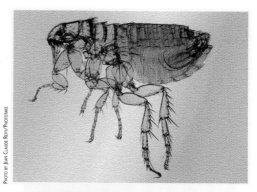

Photo by Jean Claude Revy/Phototake

EN GARDE: CATCHING FLEAS OFF GUARD!

Consider the following ways to arm yourself against fleas:

- Add a small amount of pennyroyal or eucalyptus oil to your dog's bath. These natural remedies repel fleas.
- Supplement your dog's food with fresh garlic (minced or grated) and a hearty amount of brewer's yeast, both of which ward off fleas.
- Use a flea comb on your dog daily. Submerge fleas in a cup of bleach to kill them quickly.
- Confine the dog to only a few rooms to limit the spread of fleas in the home.
- Vacuum daily...and get all of the crevices! Dispose of the bag every few days until the problem is under control.
- Wash your dog's bedding daily. Cover cushions where your dog sleeps with towels, and wash the towels often.

A LOOK AT FLEAS

Fleas have been around for millions of years and have adapted to changing host animals. They are able to go through a complete life cycle in less than one month or they can extend their lives to almost two years by remaining as pupae or cocoons. They do not need blood or any other food for up to 20 months.

They have been measured as being able to jump 300,000 times and can jump 150 times their length in any direction, including straight up. Those are just a few of the reasons why they are so successful in infesting a dog!

THE LIFE CYCLE OF THE FLEA

ggs

Larvae

Pupa

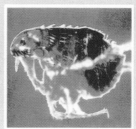

Adult

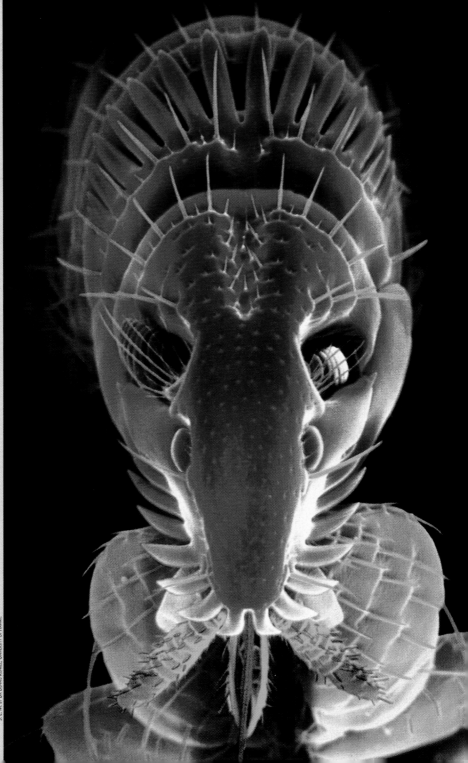

A scanning electron micrograph of a dog or cat flea, *Ctenocephalides,* magnified more than 100x. This image has been colorized for effect.

S. E. M. BY DR. DENNIS KUNKEL, UNIVERSITY OF HAWAII.

the dog. Traditionally, this would be in the form of a collar or a spray, but more recent innovations include digestible insecticides that poison the fleas when they ingest the dog's blood. Alternatively, there are drops that, when placed on the back of the animal's neck, spread throughout the fur and skin to kill adult fleas.

INSECT GROWTH REGULATOR (IGR)

Two types of products should be used when treating fleas—a product to treat the pet and a product to treat the home. Adult fleas represent less than 1% of the flea population. The pre-adult fleas (eggs, larvae and pupae) represent more than 99% of the flea population and are found in the environment; it is in the case of pre-adult fleas that products containing an Insect Growth Regulator (IGR) should be used in the home.

IGRs are a new class of compounds used to prevent the development of insects. They do not kill the insect outright, but instead use the insect's biology against it to stop it from completing its growth. Products that contain methoprene are the world's first and leading IGRs. Used to control fleas and other insects, this type of IGR will stop flea larvae from developing and protect the house for up to seven months.

DID YOU KNOW?

Never mix flea control products without first consulting your vet. Some products can become toxic when combined with others and can cause fatal consequences.

TICKS AND MITES

Though not as common as fleas, ticks and mites are found all over the tropical and temperate world. They don't bite, like fleas; they harpoon. They dig their sharp proboscis (nose) into the dog's skin and drink the blood. Their only food and drink is dog's blood. Dogs can get Lyme disease, Rocky Mountain spotted fever (normally found in the US only), paralysis and many other diseases from ticks and mites. They may live where fleas are found and they like to hide in cracks or seams in walls wherever dogs live. They are controlled the same way fleas are controlled.

The dog tick, *Dermacentor variabilis*, may well be the most common dog tick in many geographical areas, especially those areas where the climate is hot and humid. Most dog ticks

A brown dog tick, *Rhipicephalus sanguineus*, is an uncommon but annoying tick found on dogs.

PHOTO BY CAROLINA BIOLOGICAL SUPPLY/PHOTOTAKE

The head of a
dog tick,
*Dermacentor
variabilis,*
enlarged and
colorized for
effect.

Photo by Dr Dennis Kunkel, University of Hawaii

have life expectancies of a week
to six months, depending upon
climatic conditions. They can
neither jump nor fly, but they can
crawl slowly and can range up to
5 metres (16 feet) to reach a
sleeping or unsuspecting dog.

Human lice look
like dog lice;
the two are
closely related.

Photo by Dwight R Kuhn

MANGE
Mites cause a skin irritation called
mange. Some mites are
contagious, like *Cheyletiella,* ear
mites, scabies and
chiggers. Mites that
cause ear-mite
infestations
are usually
controlled
with

DEER TICK CROSSING
The great outdoors may be fun for
your dog, but it also is an home to
dangerous ticks. Deer ticks carry a
bacterium known as *Borrelia
burgdorferi* and are most active in the
autumn and spring. When infections
are caught early, penicillin and
tetracycline are effective antibiotics,
but, if left untreated, the bacteria may
cause neurological, kidney and cardiac
problems as well as long-term trouble
with walking and painful joints.

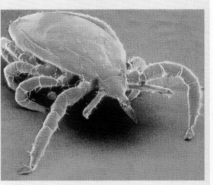

Lindane, which can only be
administered by a vet, followed by
Tresaderm at home. It is essential
that your dog be treated for
mange as quickly as possible
because some forms of mange are
transmissible to people.

Opposite page:
The dog tick, *Dermacentor variabilis,* is probably the
most common tick found on dogs. Look at the strength
in its eight legs! No wonder it's hard to detach them.

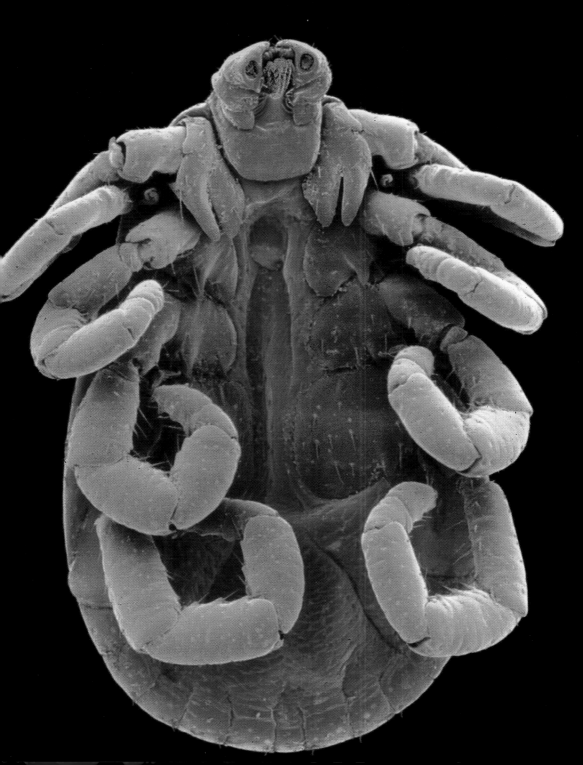

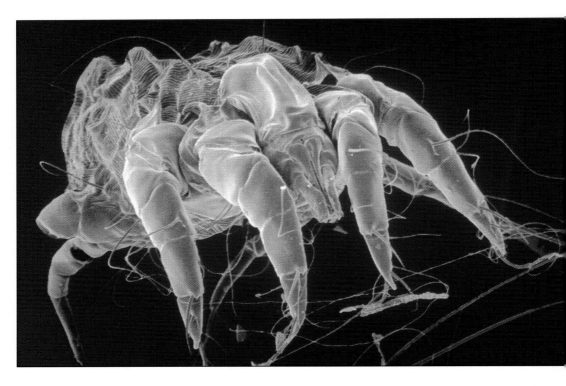

The mange mite, Psoroptes bovis.

INTERNAL PARASITES

Most animals—fishes, birds and mammals, including dogs and humans—have worms and other parasites that live inside their bodies. According to Dr Herbert R Axelrod, the fish pathologist, there are two kinds of parasites: dumb and smart. The smart parasites live in peaceful cooperation with their hosts (symbiosis), while the dumb parasites kill their hosts. Most of the worm infections are relatively easy to control. If they are not controlled, they weaken the host dog to the point that other medical problems occur, but they do not kill the host as dumb parasites would.

ROUNDWORMS

The roundworms that infect dogs are known scientifically as *Toxocara canis*. They live in the dog's intestines. The worms shed eggs continually. It has been estimated that a dog produces about 150 grammes of faeces every day. Each gramme of faeces averages 10,000–12,000 eggs of roundworms. There are no known areas in which dogs roam that do not contain roundworm eggs. The greatest danger of roundworms is

ROUNDWORMS

Average-size dogs can pass 1,360,000 roundworm eggs every day. For example, if there were only 1 million dogs in the world, the world would be saturated with 1,300 metric tonnes of dog faeces. These faeces would contain 15,000,000,000 roundworm eggs.

Up to 31% of home gardens and children's play boxes in the US contain roundworm eggs.

Flushing dog's faeces down the toilet is not a safe practice because the usual sewage treatments do not destroy roundworm eggs.

Infected puppies start shedding roundworm eggs at 3 weeks of age. They can be infected by their mother's milk.

The roundworm *Rhabditis* can infect both dogs and humans.

that they infect people too! It is wise to have your dog tested regularly for roundworms.

Pigs also have roundworm infections that can be passed to humans and dogs. The typical roundworm parasite is called *Ascaris lumbricoides.*

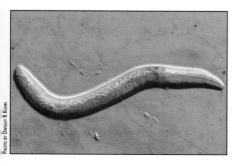

DEWORMING

Ridding your puppy of worms is *very important* because certain worms that puppies carry, such as tapeworms and roundworms, can infect humans.

Breeders initiate deworming programmes at or about four weeks of age. The routine is repeated every two or three weeks until the puppy is three months old. The breeder from whom you obtained your puppy should provide you with the complete details of the deworming programme.

Your veterinary surgeon can prescribe and monitor the programme of deworming for you. The usual programme is treating the puppy every 15–20 days until the puppy is positively worm-free. It is advised that you only treat your puppy with drugs that are recommended professionally.

The common roundworm, *Ascaris lumbricoides.*

Left: *Ancylostoma caninum* are uncommonly found in pet or show dogs in Britain.

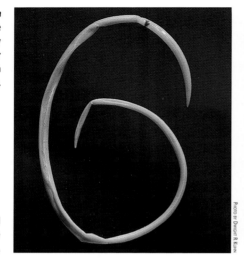

Right: Male and female hookworms.

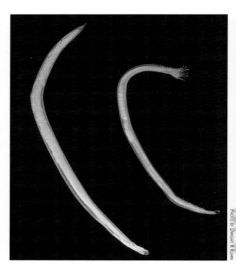

HOOKWORMS

The worm *Ancylostoma caninum* is commonly called the dog hookworm. It is also dangerous to humans and cats. It has teeth by which it attaches itself to the intestines of the dog. It changes the site of its attachment about six times a day and the dog loses blood from each detachment, possibly causing iron-deficiency anaemia. Hookworms are easily purged from the dog with many medications. Milbemycin oxime, which also serves as an heartworm preventative in Collies, can be used for this purpose.

In Britain the 'temperate climate' hookworm (*Uncinaria stenocephala*) is rarely found in pet or show dogs, but can occur in hunting packs, racing Greyhounds and sheepdogs because the worms can be prevalent wherever dogs are exercised regularly on grassland.

TAPEWORMS

There are many species of tapeworm, all of which are carried by fleas! The dog eats the flea and starts the tapeworm cycle. Humans can also be infected with tapeworms—so don't eat fleas! Fleas are so small that your dog could pass them onto your hands, your plate or your food and thus make it possible for you to ingest a flea that is carrying tapeworm eggs.

The infective stage of the hookworm larva.

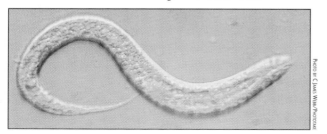

TAPEWORMS

Humans, rats, squirrels, foxes, coyotes, wolves and domestic dogs are all susceptible to tapeworm infection. Except in humans, tapeworms are usually not a fatal infection. Infected individuals can harbour 1000 parasitic worms.

Tapeworms have two sexes—male and female (many other worms have only one sex—male and female in the same worm).

If dogs eat infected rats or mice, they get the tapeworm disease. One month after attaching to a dog's intestine, the worm starts shedding eggs. These eggs are infective immediately. Infective eggs can live for a few months without an host animal.

While tapeworm infection is not life-threatening in dogs (smart parasite!), it can be the cause of a very serious liver disease for humans. About 50 percent of the humans infected with *Echinococcus multilocularis*, a type of tapeworm that causes alveolar hydatis, perish.

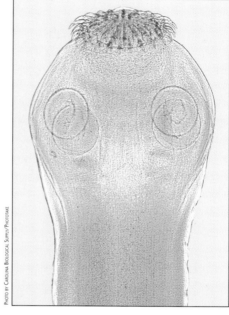

PHOTO BY CAROLINA BIOLOGICAL SUPPLY/PHOTOTAKE

The head and rostellum (the round prominence on the scolex) of a tapeworm, which infects dogs and humans.

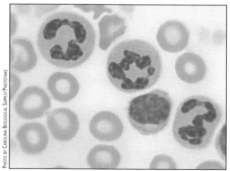

PHOTO BY CAROLINA BIOLOGICAL SUPPLY/PHOTOTAKE

Magnified heartworm larvae, *Dirofilaria immitis*.

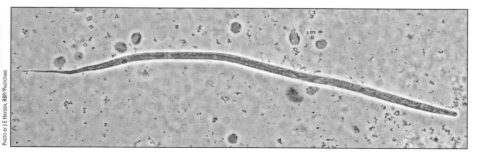

PHOTO BY J E HAYDEN, RBP/PHOTOTAKE

Heartworm, *Dirofilaria immitis*.

HEARTWORMS

Heartworms are thin, extended worms up to 30 cms (12 ins) long, which live in a dog's heart and the major blood vessels surrounding it. Dogs may have up to 200 worms. Symptoms may be loss of energy, loss of appetite, coughing, the development of a pot belly and anaemia.

Heartworms are transmitted by mosquitoes. The mosquito drinks the blood of an infected dog and takes in larvae with the blood. The larvae, called microfilaria, develop within the body of the mosquito and are passed on to the next dog bitten after the larvae mature. It takes two to three weeks for the larvae to develop to the infective stage within the body of the mosquito. Dogs should be treated at about six weeks of age, and maintained on a prophylactic dose given monthly.

Blood testing for heartworms is not necessarily indicative of how seriously your dog is infected. This is a dangerous disease. Although heartworm is a problem for dogs in America, Australia, Asia and Central Europe, dogs in the United Kingdom are not currently affected by heartworm.

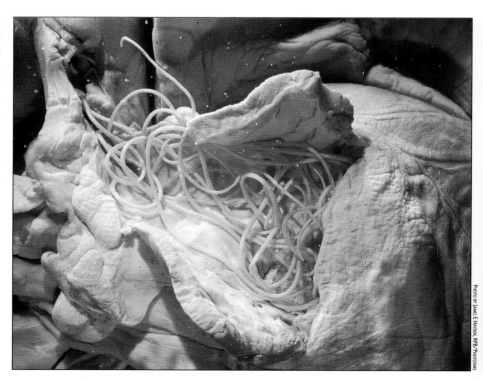

The heart of a dog infected with canine heartworm, *Dirofilaria immitis.*

PHOTO BY JAMES E HAYDEN, RPB/PHOTOTAKE

Number-One Killer Disease in Dogs: CANCER

In every age there is a word associated with a disease or plague that causes humans to shudder. In the 21st century, that word is 'cancer.' Just as cancer is the leading cause of death in humans, it claims nearly half the lives of dogs that die from a natural disease as well as half the dogs that die over the age of ten years.

Described as a genetic disease, cancer becomes a greater risk as the dog ages. Veterinary surgeons and dog owners have become increasingly aware of the threat of cancer to dogs. Statistics reveal that one dog in every five will develop cancer, the most common of which is skin cancer. Many cancers, including prostate, ovarian and breast cancer, can be avoided by spaying and neutering our dogs by the age of six months.

Early detection of cancer can save or extend your dog's life, so it is absolutely vital for owners to have their dogs examined by a qualified veterinary surgeon or oncologist immediately upon detection of any abnormality. Certain dietary guidelines have also proven to reduce the onset and spread of cancer. Foods based on fish rather than beef, due to the presence of Omega-3 fatty acids, are recommended. Other amino acids such as glutamine have significant benefits for canines, particularly those breeds that show a greater susceptibility to cancer.

Cancer management and treatments promise hope for future generations of canines. Since the disease is genetic, breeders should never breed a dog whose parents, grandparents and any related siblings have developed cancer. It is difficult to know whether to exclude an otherwise healthy dog from a breeding programme as the disease does not manifest itself until the dog's senior years.

RECOGNISE CANCER WARNING SIGNS

Since early detection can possibly rescue your dog from becoming a cancer statistic, it is essential for owners to recognise the possible signs and seek the assistance of a qualified professional.

- Abnormal bumps or lumps that continue to grow
- Bleeding or discharge from any body cavity
- Persistent stiffness or lameness
- Recurrent sores or sores that do not heal
- Inappetence
- Breathing difficulties
- Weight loss
- Bad breath or odours
- General malaise and fatigue
- Eating and swallowing problems
- Difficulty urinating and defecating

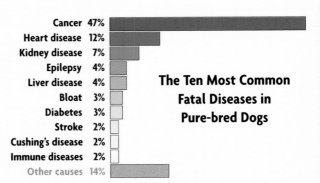

Disease	Percentage
Cancer	47%
Heart disease	12%
Kidney disease	7%
Epilepsy	4%
Liver disease	4%
Bloat	3%
Diabetes	3%
Stroke	2%
Cushing's disease	2%
Immune diseases	2%
Other causes	14%

The Ten Most Common Fatal Diseases in Pure-bred Dogs

HOMEOPATHY:

an alternative
to conventional
medicine

'Less is Most'

Using this principle, the strength
of an homeopathic remedy is
measured by the number of
serial dilutions that were
undertaken to create it. The
greater the number of serial
dilutions, the greater the
strength of the homeopathic
remedy. The potency of a
remedy that has been made by
making a dilution of 1 part in
100 parts (or 1/100) is 1c or 1cH.
If this remedy is subjected to a
series of further dilutions, each
one being 1/100, a more dilute
and stronger remedy is
produced. If the remedy is
diluted in this way six times, it is
called 6c or 6cH. A dilution of 6c
is 1 part in 1,000,000,000,000. In
general, higher potencies in
more frequent doses are better
for acute symptoms and lower
potencies in more infrequent
doses are more useful for
chronic, long-standing problems.

CURING OUR DOGS NATURALLY

Holistic medicine means treating
the whole animal as a unique,
perfect living being. Generally,
holistic treatments do not suppress
the symptoms that the body
naturally produces, as do most
medications prescribed by conventional doctors and vets. Holistic
methods seek to cure disease by
regaining balance and harmony in
the patient's environment. Some of
these methods include use of
nutritional therapy, herbs, flower
essences, aromatherapy, acupunc-
ture, massage, chiropractic and, of
course, the most popular holistic
approach, homeopathy.

Homeopathy is a theory or
system of treating illness with
small doses of substances which, if
administered in larger quantities,
would produce the symptoms that
the patient already has. This
approach is often described as 'like
cures like.' Although modern
veterinary medicine is geared
toward the 'quick fix,' homeopathy
relies on the belief that, given the
time, the body is able to heal itself
and return to its natural, healthy
state.

Choosing a remedy to cure a
problem in our dogs is the difficult
part of homeopathy. Consult with
your veterinary surgeon for a
professional diagnosis of your dog's
symptoms. Often these symptoms

require immediate conventional care. If your vet is willing, and knowledgeable, you may attempt an homeopathic remedy. Be aware that cortisone prevents homeopathic remedies from working. There are hundreds of possibilities and combinations to cure many problems in dogs, from basic physical problems such as excessive moulting, fleas or other parasites, unattractive doggy odour, bad breath, upset tummy, obesity, dry, oily or dull coat, diarrhoea, ear problems or eye discharge (including tears and dry or mucousy matter), to behavioural abnormalities, such as fear of loud noises, habitual licking, poor appetite, excessive barking and various phobias. From alumina to zincum metallicum, the remedies span the planet and the imagination…from flowers and weeds to chemicals, insect droppings, diesel smoke and volcanic ash.

Using 'Like to Treat Like'

Unlike conventional medicines that suppress symptoms, homeopathic remedies treat illnesses with small doses of substances that, if administered in larger quantities, would produce the symptoms that the patient already has. While the same homeopathic remedy can be used to treat different symptoms in different dogs, here are some interesting remedies and their uses.

Apis Mellifica
(made from honey bee venom) can be used for allergies or to reduce swelling that occurs in acutely infected kidneys.

Diesel Smoke
can be used to help control travel sickness.

Calcarea Fluorica
(made from calcium fluoride, which helps harden bone structure) can be useful in treating hard lumps in tissues.

Natrum Muriaticum
(made from common salt, sodium chloride) is useful in treating thin, thirsty dogs.

Nitricum Acidum
(made from nitric acid) is used for symptoms you would expect to see from contact with acids, such as lesions, especially where the skin joins the linings of body orifices or openings such as the lips and nostrils.

Symphytum
(made from the herb Knitbone, *Symphytum officianale*) is used to encourage bones to heal.

Urtica Urens
(made from the common stinging nettle) is used in treating painful, irritating rashes.

HOMEOPATHIC REMEDIES FOR YOUR DOG

Symptom/Ailment	Possible Remedy
ALLERGIES	Apis Mellifica 30c, Astacus Fluviatilis 6c, Pulsatilla 30c, Urtica Urens 6c
ALOPAECIA	Alumina 30c, Lycopodium 30c, Sepia 30c, Thallium 6c
ANAL GLANDS (BLOCKED)	Hepar Sulphuris Calcareum 30c, Sanicula 6c, Silicea 6c
ARTHRITIS	Rhus Toxicodendron 6c, Bryonia Alba 6c
CATARACT	Calcarea Carbonica 6c, Conium Maculatum 6c, Phosphorus 30c, Silicea 30c
CONSTIPATION	Alumina 6c, Carbo Vegetabilis 30c, Graphites 6c, Nitricum Acidum 30c, Silicea 6c
COUGHING	Aconitum Napellus 6c, Belladonna 30c, Hyoscyamus Niger 30c, Phosphorus 30c
DIARRHOEA	Arsenicum Album 30c, Aconitum Napellus 6c, Chamomilla 30c, Mercurius Corrosivus 30c
DRY EYE	Zincum Metallicum 30c
EAR PROBLEMS	Aconitum Napellus 30c, Belladonna 30c, Hepar Sulphuris 30c, Tellurium 30c, Psorinum 200c
EYE PROBLEMS	Borax 6c, Aconitum Napellus 30c, Graphites 6c, Staphysagria 6c, Thuja Occidentalis 30c
GLAUCOMA	Aconitum Napellus 30c, Apis Mellifica 6c, Phosphorus 30c
HEAT STROKE	Belladonna 30c, Gelsemium Sempervirens 30c, Sulphur 30c
HICCOUGHS	Cinchona Deficinalis 6c
HIP DYSPLASIA	Colocynthis 6c, Rhus Toxicodendron 6c, Bryonia Alba 6c
INCONTINENCE	Argentum Nitricum 6c, Causticum 30c, Conium Maculatum 30c, Pulsatilla 30c, Sepia 30c
INSECT BITES	Apis Mellifica 30c, Cantharis 30c, Hypericum Perforatum 6c, Urtica Urens 30c
ITCHING	Alumina 30c, Arsenicum Album 30c, Carbo Vegetabilis 30c, Hypericum Perforatum 6c, Mezerium 6c, Sulphur 30c
KENNEL COUGH	Drosera 6c, Ipecacuanha 30c
MASTITIS	Apis Mellifica 30c, Belladonna 30c, Urtica Urens 1m
PATELLAR LUXATION	Gelsemium Sempervirens 6c, Rhus Toxicodendron 6c
PENIS PROBLEMS	Aconitum Napellus 30c, Hepar Sulphuris Calcareum 30c, Pulsatilla 30c, Thuja Occidentalis 6c
PUPPY TEETHING	Calcarea Carbonica 6c, Chamomilla 6c, Phytolacca 6c
TRAVEL SICKNESS	Cocculus 6c, Petroleum 6c

Recognising a Sick Dog

Unlike colicky babies and cranky children, our canine charges cannot tell us when they are feeling ill. Therefore, there are a number of signs that owners can identify to know that their dogs are not feeling well.

Take note for physical manifestations such as:

- unusual, bad odour, including bad breath
- excessive moulting
- wax in the ears, chronic ear irritation
- oily, flaky, dull haircoat
- mucous, tearing or similar discharge in the eyes
- fleas or mites
- mucous in stool, diarrhoea
- sensitivity to petting or handling
- licking at paws, scratching face, etc.

Keep an eye out for behavioural changes as well including:

- lethargy, idleness
- lack of patience or general irritability
- lack of appetite, digestive problems
- phobias (fear of people, loud noises, etc.)
- strange behaviour, suspicion, fear
- coprophagia
- more frequent barking
- whimpering, crying

Get Well Soon

You don't need a DVR or a BVMA to provide good TLC to your sick or recovering dog, but you do need to pay attention to some details that normally wouldn't bother him. The following tips will aid Fido's recovery and get him back on his paws again:

- Keep his space free of irritating smells, like heavy perfumes and air fresheners.
- Rest is the best medicine! Avoid harsh lighting that will prevent your dog from sleeping. Shade him from bright sunlight during the day and dim the lights in the evening.
- Keep the noise level down. Animals are more sensitive to sound when they are sick.

- Be attentive to any necessary temperature adjustments. A dog with a fever needs a cool room and cold liquids. A bitch that is whelping or recovering from surgery will be more comfortable in a warm room, consuming warm liquids and food.
- You wouldn't send a sick child back to school early, so don't rush your dog back into a full routine until he seems absolutely ready.

Your Veteran
SCHNAUZER

The term *old* is a qualitative term. For dogs, as well as for their masters, old is relative. Certainly we can all distinguish between a puppy Schnauzer and an adult Schnauzer—there are the obvious physical traits, such as size, appearance and facial furnishings, as well as personality traits. Puppies and young dogs like to play with children. Children's natural exuberance is a good match for the seemingly endless energy of young dogs. They like to run, jump, chase and retrieve. When dogs grow older and cease their interaction with children, they are often thought of as being too old to keep pace with the young folk. On the other hand, if a Schnauzer is only exposed to older people or quieter lifestyles, his life will normally be less active and the decrease in his activity level as he ages will not be as obvious.

If people live to be 100 years old, dogs live to be 20 years old. While this might seem like a good rule of thumb, it is very inaccurate. When trying to compare dog years to human years, you cannot make a generalisation about all dogs. With excellent-quality dog food readily available, and with regular veterinary care, the average longevity seems to be around 14 years. It is not unusual for the Schnauzer to live to 16 or 17 years of age. Since the breed is blest with good health, and relative freedom from hereditary problems, most Schnauzers die from 'old age' (if that exists!) rather than from health problems.

Generally, the first three years of a dog's life are like seven times that of a comparable human. That means a 3-year-old dog is like a 21-year-old human. As the curve of comparison shows, there is no hard and fast rule for comparing dog and human ages. Small breeds tend to live longer than large breeds, some breeds' adolescent periods last longer than others' and some breeds experience rapid periods of growth. The comparison is made even more difficult, for, likewise, not all humans age at the same rate...and human females live longer than human males.

WHAT TO LOOK FOR IN SENIORS
Most veterinary surgeons and behaviourists use the seven-year mark as the time to consider a dog a 'senior' or 'veteran,' though nine

CDS: COGNITIVE DYSFUNCTION SYNDROME
'OLD-DOG SYNDROME'

There are many ways to evaluate old-dog syndrome. Veterinary surgeons have defined CDS (cognitive dysfunction syndrome) as the gradual deterioration of cognitive abilities. These are indicated by changes in the dog's behaviour. When a dog changes its routine response, and maladies have been eliminated as the cause of these behavioural changes, then CDS is the usual diagnosis.

More than half the dogs over eight years old suffer from some form of CDS. The older the dog, the more chance it has of suffering from CDS. In humans, doctors often dismiss the CDS behavioural changes as part of 'winding down.'

There are four major signs of CDS: the dog has frequent toilet accidents inside the home, sleeps much more or much less than normal, acts confused and fails to respond to social stimuli.

SYMPTOMS OF CDS

FREQUENT TOILET ACCIDENTS
- *Urinates in the house.*
- *Defecates in the house.*
- *Doesn't signal that he wants to go out.*

SLEEP PATTERNS
- *Moves much more slowly.*
- *Sleeps more than normal during the day.*
- *Sleeps less during the night.*

CONFUSION
- *Goes outside and just stands there.*
- *Appears confused with a faraway look in his eyes.*
- *Hides more often.*
- *Doesn't recognise friends.*
- *Doesn't come when called.*
- *Walks around listlessly and without a destination.*

FAILS TO RESPOND TO SOCIAL STIMULI
- *Comes to people less frequently, whether called or not.*
- *Doesn't tolerate petting for more than a short time.*
- *Doesn't come to the door when you return home.*

or ten years is more accurate for the Schnauzer. Neither 'senior' nor 'veteran' implies that the dog is geriatric and has begun to fail in mind and body. Ageing is essentially a slowing process. Humans readily admit that they feel a difference in their activity level from age 20 to 30, and then from 30 to 40, etc. By treating the older dog as a senior, owners are able to implement certain therapeutic and preventative medical strategies with the help of their veterinary surgeons.

A senior-care programme should include at least two veterinary visits per year and screening sessions to determine the dog's health status, as well as nutritional counselling. Veterinary surgeons determine the senior dog's health status through a blood smear for a complete blood count, serum chemistry profile with electrolytes, urinalysis, blood pressure check, electrocardiogram, ocular tonometry (pressure on the eyeball) and dental prophylaxis.

Such an extensive programme for senior dogs is well advised before owners start to see the obvious physical signs of ageing, such as slower and inhibited movement, greying, increased sleep/nap periods and disinterest in play and other activity. This preventative programme promises a longer, healthier life for the ageing dog. Among the physical problems common in ageing dogs

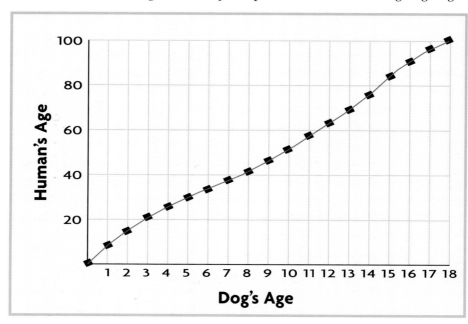

NOTICING THE SYMPTOMS

The symptoms listed below are symptoms that gradually appear and become more noticeable. They are not life-threatening; however, the symptoms below are to be taken very seriously and warrant a discussion with your veterinary surgeon:

• Your dog cries and whimpers when he moves, and he stops running completely.

• Convulsions start or become more serious and frequent. The usual convulsion (spasm) is when the dog stiffens and starts to tremble, being unable or unwilling to move. The seizure usually lasts for 5 to 30 minutes.

• Your dog drinks more water and urinates more frequently. Wetting and bowel accidents take place indoors without warning.

• Vomiting becomes more and more frequent.

are the loss of sight and hearing, arthritis, kidney and liver failure, diabetes mellitus, heart disease and Cushing's disease (an hormonal disease).

In addition to the physical manifestations discussed, there are some behavioural changes and problems related to ageing dogs. Dogs suffering from hearing or vision loss, dental discomfort or arthritis can become aggressive. Likewise, the near-deaf and/or blind dog may be startled more easily and react in an unexpectedly aggressive manner. Seniors suffering from senility can become more impatient and irritable. Housesoiling accidents are associated with loss of mobility, kidney problems and loss of sphincter control as well as plaque accumulation, physiological brain changes and reactions to medications.

Older dogs, just like young puppies, suffer from separation anxiety, which can lead to excessive barking, whining, housesoiling and destructive behaviour. Seniors may become fearful of everyday sounds, such as vacuum cleaners, heaters, thunder and passing traffic. Some dogs have difficulty sleeping, due to discomfort, the need for frequent toilet visits and the like.

Owners should avoid spoiling the older dog with too many fatty treats. Obesity is a common problem in older dogs and subtracts years from their lives. Keep the senior dog as trim as possible, since excessive weight puts additional stress on the body's vital organs. Some breeders recommend supplementing the diet with foods high in fibre and lower in calories. Adding fresh vegetables and marrow broth to the senior's diet makes a tasty, low-calorie, low-fat supplement. Vets also offer speciality diets for senior dogs that are worth exploring.

Your dog, as he nears his twilight years, needs your patience and good care more than ever. Never punish an older dog for an accident or abnormal behaviour. For all the years of love, protection and companionship that your dog has provided, he deserves special attention and courtesies. The older dog may need to relieve himself at 3 a.m. because he can no longer hold it for eight hours. Older dogs may not be able to remain crated for more than two or three hours. It may be time to give up a sofa or chair to your old friend. Although he may not seem as enthusiastic about your attention and petting, he does appreciate the considerations you offer as he gets older.

Your Schnauzer does not understand why his world is slowing down. Owners must make their dogs' transition into their golden years as pleasant and rewarding as possible.

WHAT TO DO WHEN THE TIME COMES

You are never fully prepared to make a rational decision about putting your dog to sleep. It is very obvious that you love your Schnauzer or you would not be reading this book. Putting a beloved dog to sleep is extremely difficult. It is a decision that must be made with your veterinary surgeon.

You are usually forced to make the decision when your dog experiences one or more life-threatening symptoms that have become serious enough for you to seek medical (veterinary) help. If the prognosis of the malady indicates that the end is near and that your beloved pet will only continue to suffer and experience no enjoyment for the balance of its life, then euthanasia is the right choice.

WHAT IS EUTHANASIA?
Euthanasia derives from the Greek, meaning *good death*. In other words, it means the planned, painless killing of a dog suffering from a painful, incurable condition, or who is so aged that it cannot walk, see, eat or control its excretory functions. Euthanasia is usually accomplished by injection with an overdose of anaesthesia or a barbiturate. Aside from the prick of the needle, the experience is usually painless.

EUTHANASIA
Euthanasia must be performed by a licensed veterinary surgeon. There also may be societies for the prevention of cruelty to animals in your area. They often offer this service upon a vet's recommendation.

MAKING THE DECISION

The decision to euthanise your dog is never easy. The days during which the dog becomes ill and the end occurs can be unusually stressful for you. If this is your first experience with the death of a loved one, you may need the comfort dictated by your religious beliefs. If you are the head of the family and have children, you should have involved them in the decision of putting your Schnauzer to sleep. Usually your dog can be maintained on drugs for a few days in order to give you ample time to make a decision. During this time, talking with members of your family or with people who have lived through the same experience can ease the burden of your inevitable decision.

THE FINAL RESTING PLACE

Dogs can have some of the same privileges as humans. The remains of your beloved dog can be buried in a pet cemetery, which is generally expensive. Alternatively, your dog can be cremated individually and the ashes returned to you. A less expensive option is mass cremation, although, of course, the ashes cannot then be returned. Vets can usually arrange the cremation on your behalf. The cost of these options should always be discussed frankly and openly with your veterinary surgeon. In Britain, if your dog has died at the surgery, the vet legally cannot allow you to take your dog's body home because it is unlawful to bury an animal's remains in your garden.

GETTING ANOTHER DOG?

The grief of losing your beloved dog will be as lasting as the grief of losing a human friend or relative. In most cases, if your dog died of old age it had slowed down considerably. Do you want a new Schnauzer puppy to replace it? Or are you better off finding a more mature Schnauzer, say two to three years of age, which will usually be house-trained and will have an already developed personality. In this case, you can find out if you like each other after a few hours of being together.

The decision is, of course, your own. Do you want another Schnauzer or perhaps a different breed so as to avoid comparison with your beloved friend? Most people usually buy the same breed because they know (and love) the characteristics of that breed. Then, too, they often know people who have the same breed and perhaps they are lucky enough that one of their friends expects a litter soon. What could be better?

Showing Your
SCHNAUZER

When you purchase your Schnauzer, you will make it clear to the breeder whether you want one just as a loveable companion and pet, or if you hope to be buying a Schnauzer with show prospects. No reputable breeder will sell you a young puppy and tell you that it is *definitely* of show quality, for so much can go wrong during the early months of a puppy's development. If you plan to show, what you will hopefully have acquired is a puppy with 'show potential.'

To the novice, exhibiting a Schnauzer in the show ring may look easy, but it takes a lot of hard work and devotion to do top winning at a show such as the prestigious Crufts Dog Show, not to mention a little luck too!

The first concept that the canine novice learns when watching a dog show is that each dog first competes against members of its own breed. Once the judge has selected the best member of each breed (Best of Breed), provided that the show is judged on a Group system, that chosen dog will compete with other dogs in its group. Finally, the best of each group will compete for Best in Show and Reserve Best in Show.

The second concept that you must understand is that the dogs are not actually compared against one another. The judge compares each dog against its breed standard, which is the approved description of the ideal specimen of the breed. While some early breed standards were indeed based on specific dogs that were famous or popular, many dedicated enthusiasts say that a perfect specimen, as described in the standard, has never walked into a show ring, has never been bred and, to the woe of dog breeders around the globe, does not exist. Breeders attempt to get as close to this ideal as possible with every litter, but theoretically the 'perfect' dog is so elusive that it is impossible. (And if the 'perfect' dog were born, breeders and judges would never agree that it was indeed 'perfect.')

If you are interested in exploring the world of dog showing, your best bet is to join your local breed club. These clubs often host both Championship and Open Shows, and sometimes Match meetings and special

INFORMATION ON CLUBS

You can get information about dog shows from kennel clubs and breed clubs:

Fédération Cynologique Internationale
14, rue Leopold II, B-6530 Thuin, Belgium
www.fci.be

The Kennel Club
1-5 Clarges St., Piccadilly, London W1Y 8AB
UK
www.the-kennel-club.org.uk

American Kennel Club
5580 Centerview Dr., Raleigh, NC 27606-3390
USA
www.akc.org

Canadian Kennel Club
89 Skyway Ave., Suite 100, Etobicoke,
Ontario
M9W 6R4 Canada
www.ckc.ca

events plus general dog registration and other basic requirements of dog ownership. Its annual show, called the Crufts Dog Show, held in Birmingham, is the largest benched show in England. Every year over 20,000 of the UK's best dogs qualify to participate in this marvellous show, which lasts four days.

The Kennel Club governs many different kinds of shows in Great Britain, Australia, South Africa and beyond. At the most competitive and prestigious of these shows, the Championship Shows, a dog can earn Challenge Certificates (CCs), and thereby become a Show Champion or a Champion. A dog must earn three Challenge Certificates under three different judges to earn the prefix of 'Sh Ch' or 'Ch.' Some breeds must also qualify in a field trial in order to gain the title of full Champion, though the Schnauzer is not one such breed. CCs are awarded to a very small percentage of the dogs competing, and dogs that are already Champions compete with others for these coveted CCs. The number of CCs awarded in any one year is based upon the total number of dogs in each breed entered for competition.

There are three types of Championship Shows: an all-breed General Championship Show for all Kennel-Club-recognised breeds; a Group

events, all of which could be of interest, even if you are only an onlooker. Clubs also send out newsletters, and some organise training days and seminars in order that people may learn more about their chosen breed. To locate the breed club closest to you, contact The Kennel Club, the ruling body for the British dog world.

The Kennel Club governs not only conformation shows but also working trials, obedience shows, agility trials and field trials. The Kennel Club furnishes the rules and regulations for all of these

Championship Show, which is limited to breeds within one of the groups; and a Breed Show, which is usually confined to a single breed. The Kennel Club determines which breeds at which Championship Shows will have the opportunity to earn CCs (or tickets). Serious exhibitors often will opt not to participate if the tickets are withheld at a particular show. This policy makes earning championships even more difficult to accomplish.

Open Shows are generally less competitive and are frequently used as 'practice shows' for young dogs. There are hundreds of Open Shows each year that can be delightful social events and are great first show experiences for the novice. Even if you're considering just watching a show to wet your paws, an Open Show is a great choice.

While Championship and Open Shows are most important for the beginner to understand, there are other types of shows in which the interested dog owner can participate. Training clubs sponsor Matches that can be entered on the day of the show for a nominal fee. In these introductory-level exhibitions, two dogs' names are pulled out of a hat and 'matched,' the winner of that match goes on to the next round and eventually only one dog is left undefeated.

Exemption Shows are much more light-hearted affairs with usually only four pedigree classes and several 'fun' classes, all of which can be entered on the day of the show. Exemption Shows are sometimes held in conjunction with small agricultural shows and the proceeds must be given to a charity. Limited Shows are also available in small number. Entry is restricted to members of the club that hosts the show, although you can usually join the club when making an entry.

Before you actually step into the ring, you would be well advised to sit back and observe the judge's ring procedure. If it is your first time in the ring, do not be over-anxious and run to the front of the line. It is much better to stand back and study how the exhibitor in front of you is performing. The judge asks each handler to 'stand' the dog, hopefully showing the dog off to his best advantage. The judge will observe the dog from a distance and from different angles, and approach the dog to check his teeth, overall structure, alertness and muscle tone, as well as consider how well the dog 'conforms' to the standard. Most importantly, the judge will have the exhibitor move the dog around the ring in some pattern that he or she should specify (another advantage to not going first, but always listen since some judges change their directions—

and the judge is always right!). Finally, the judge will give the dog one last look before moving on to the next exhibitor.

If you are not in the top three at your first show, do not be discouraged. Be patient and consistent, and you may eventually find yourself in the winning line-up. Remember that the winners were once in your shoes and have devoted many hours and much money to earn the placement. If you find that your dog is losing every time and never getting a nod, it may be time to consider a different dog sport or to just enjoy your Schnauzer as a pet.

Virtually all countries with a recognised speciality breed club (sometimes called a 'parent' club) offer show conformation competition specifically for and among Schnauzers. Under direction of the club, other special events for herding, tracking, obedience and agility may be offered as well, whether for titling or just for fun.

WORKING TRIALS

Working trials can be entered by any well-trained dog of any breed, not just Gundogs or Working dogs. Many dogs that earn the Kennel Club Good Citizen Dog award choose to participate in a working trial. There are five stakes at both Open and Championship levels: Companion Dog (CD), Utility Dog (UD), Working Dog (WD),

HOW TO ENTER A DOG SHOW
1. Obtain an entry form and show schedule from the Show Secretary.
2. Select the classes that you want to enter and complete the entry form.
3. Transfer your dog into your name at The Kennel Club. (Be sure that this matter is handled before entering.)
4. Find out how far in advance show entries must be made. Oftentimes it's more than a couple of months.

This agility exercise includes jumping over a hurdle with a removable top bar. Some Schnauzers are superior jumpers and take to this exercise with exceptional grace.

Tracking Dog (TD) and Patrol Dog (PD). As in conformation shows, dogs compete against a standard and, if the dog reaches the qualifying mark, it obtains a certificate. The exercises are divided into groups, and the dog must achieve at least 70 percent of the allotted score for each exercise in order to qualify. If the dog achieves 80 percent in the Open level, it receives a Certificate of Merit (COM); in the Championship level, it receives a Qualifying Certificate. At the CD stake, dogs must participate in four groups: Control, Stay, Agility and Search (Retrieve and Nosework). At the next three levels, UD, WD and TD, there are only three groups: Control, Agility and Nosework.

The Agility exercises consist of three jumps: a vertical scale up a six-foot wall of planks; a clear jump over a basic three-foot hurdle with a removable top bar; and a long jump across angled planks stretching nine feet.

To earn the UD, WD and TD, dogs must track approximately one-half mile for articles laid from one-half hour to three hours previously. Tracks consist of turns and legs, and fresh ground is used for each participant. The fifth stake, PD, involves teaching manwork, which is not recommended for every breed.

AGILITY TRIALS

Agility trials began in the United Kingdom in 1977 and have since spread around the world, especially to the United States, where they are very popular. The handler directs his dog over obstacle courses that include jumps (such as those used in the working trials), as well as tyres, the dog walk, weave poles, pipe tunnels, collapsed tunnels, etc. The Kennel Club requires that dogs not be trained for agility until they are 12 months old. This dog sport is great fun for dog and owner, and interested owners should join a training club that has obstacles and experienced agility handlers who can introduce you and your dog to the 'ropes' (and tyres, tunnels, etc.).

FÉDÉRATION CYNOLOGIQUE INTERNATIONALE

Established in 1911, the Fédération Cynologique Internationale (FCI) represents the 'world kennel club.' This international body brings uniformity to the breeding, judging and showing of pure-bred dogs. Although the FCI originally included only five European nations: France, Germany, Austria, the Netherlands and Belgium (which remains its headquarters), the organisation today embraces nations on six continents and recognises well over 300 breeds of pure-bred dog.

FCI sponsors both national and international shows. The hosting country determines the judging system and breed standards are always based on the breed's country of origin. Dogs from every country can participate in these impressive canine spectacles, the largest of which is the

Argenta's Emmett from Sweden, proudly displaying his curly tail. Sweden forbids tail docking and ear cropping.

World Dog Show, hosted in a different country each year.

There are three titles attainable through the FCI: the International Champion, which is the most prestigious; the International Beauty Champion, which is based on aptitude certificates in different countries; and the International Trial Champion, which is based on achievement in obedience trials in different countries. A title at an FCI show

Ch Argenta's Dutchman is an accomplished Schnauzer, who displays a tail of similar length to Argenta's Emmett, though it is not as tightly curled.

requires a dog to win three CACs (*Certificats d'Aptitude au Championnat*), at regional or club shows under three different judges who are breed specialists. The title of International Champion is gained by winning four CACIBs (*Certificats d'Aptitude au Championnat International de Beauté*), which are offered only at international shows, with at least a one-year lapse between the first and fourth award.

The FCI is divided into ten groups. At the World Dog Show, the following classes are offered for each breed: Puppy Class (6–9 months), Youth Class (9–18 months), Open Class (15 months or older) and Champion Class. A dog can be awarded a classification of Excellent, Very Good, Good, Sufficient and Not Sufficient. Puppies can be awarded classifications of Very Promising, Promising or Not Promising. Four placements are made in each class. After all sexes and classes are judged, a Best of Breed is selected. Other special groups and classes may also be shown. Each exhibitor showing a dog receives a written evaluation from the judge.

Besides the World Dog Show and other all-breed shows, you can exhibit your dog at speciality shows held by different breed clubs. Speciality shows may have their own regulations.

As a Schnauzer owner, you have selected your dog so that you and your loved ones can have a companion, a protector, a friend and a four-legged family member. You invest time, money and effort to care for and train the family's new charge. Of course, this chosen canine behaves perfectly! Well, perfectly like a *dog*.

THINK LIKE A DOG

Dogs do not think like humans, nor do humans think like dogs, though we try. Unfortunately, a dog is incapable of comprehending how humans think, so the responsibility falls on the owner to adopt a proper canine mindset. Dogs cannot rationalise, and dogs exist in the present moment. Many dog owners make the mistake in training of thinking that they can reprimand their dog for something he did a while ago. Basically, you cannot even reprimand a dog for something he did 20 seconds ago! Either catch him in the act or forget it! It is a waste of your and your dog's time—in his mind, you are reprimanding him for whatever he is doing at that moment.

The following behavioural problems represent some which owners most commonly encounter. Every dog is unique and every situation is unique. No author could purport for you to solve your Schnauzer's problems simply by reading a script. Here

NO KISSES

We all love our dogs and our dogs love us. They show their love and affection by licking us. This is not a very sanitary practice, as dogs lick and sniff in some unsavoury places. Kissing your dog on the mouth is strictly forbidden, as parasites can be transmitted in this manner.

SEPARATION ANXIETY

The number of dogs that suffer from separation anxiety is on the rise as more and more pet owners find themselves at work all day. New attention is being paid to this problem, which is especially hard to diagnose since it is only evident when the dog is alone. Research is currently being done to help educate dog owners about separation anxiety and how they can help minimise this problem in their dogs.

we outline some basic 'dogspeak' so that owners' chances of solving behavioural problems are increased. Discuss bad habits with your veterinary surgeon and he/she can recommend a behavioural specialist to consult in appropriate cases. Since behavioural abnormalities are the main reason for owners abandoning their pets, we hope that you will make a valiant effort to solve your Schnauzer's problems. Patience and understanding are virtues that must dwell in every pet-loving household.

SEPARATION ANXIETY

Recognised by behaviourists as the most common form of stress for dogs, separation anxiety can also lead to destructive behaviours in your dog. It's more than your Schnauzer's howling his displeasure at your leaving the house and his being left alone. This is a normal reaction, no different from the child who cries as his mother leaves him on the first day at school. Separation anxiety is more serious. In fact, if you are constantly with your dog, he will come to expect you with him all of the time, making it even more traumatic for him when you are not there.

Obviously, you enjoy spending time with your dog, and he thrives on your love and attention. However, it should not become a dependent relationship in which he is heartbroken without you. This broken heart can also bring on destructive behaviour as well as loss of appetite, depression and lack of interest in play and interaction. Canine behaviourists have been spending much time and energy to help owners better understand the significance of this stressful condition.

One thing you can do to minimise separation anxiety is to make your entrances and exits as low-key as possible. Do not give your dog a long drawn-out goodbye, and do not overly lavish him with hugs and kisses when you return. This is giving in to the attention that he craves, and it will only make him miss it more when you are away. Another thing you can try is to give your dog a treat when you leave; this will not only keep him occupied and keep his mind off the fact that you have just left, but it will also help him associate your leaving with a pleasant experience.

You may have to accustom your dog to being left alone at intervals. Of course, when your dog starts whimpering as you approach the door, your first instinct will be to run to him and comfort him, but do not do it! Really—eventually he will adjust to your absence. His anxiety stems from being placed in an unfamiliar situation; by familiarising him with being

I'M HOME!
Dogs left alone for varying lengths of time may often react wildly when their owners return. Sometimes they run, jump, bite, chew, tear things apart, wet themselves, gobble their food or behave in very undisciplined ways. If your dog behaves in this manner upon your return home, allow him to calm down before greeting him or he will consider your attention as a reward for his antics.

AGGRESSIVE BEHAVIOUR

Dog aggression is a serious problem. NEVER give an aggressive dog to someone else. The dog will usually be more aggressive in a new situation where his leadership is unchallenged and unquestioned (in his mind).

alone, he will learn that he will survive. That is not to say you should purposely leave your dog home alone, but the dog needs to know that, while he can depend on you for his care, you do not have to be by his side 24 hours a day. Some behaviourists recommend tiring the dog out before you leave home—take him for a good long walk or engage in a game of fetch in the garden.

When the dog is alone in the house, he should be placed in his crate—another distinct advantage to crate training your dog. The crate should be placed in his

familiar happy family area, where he normally sleeps and already feels comfortable, thereby making him feel more at ease when he is alone. Be sure to give the dog a special chew toy to enjoy while he settles into his crate.

AGGRESSION

This is a problem that concerns all responsible dog owners. Aggression can be a very big problem in dogs, and, when not controlled, always becomes dangerous. An aggressive dog, no matter the size, may lunge at, bite or even attack a person or another dog. Aggressive behaviour is not to be tolerated. It is more than just inappropriate behaviour; it is painful for a family to watch their dog become unpredictable in his behaviour to the point where they are afraid of him. While not all aggressive behaviour is dangerous, growling, baring teeth, etc., can be frightening. It is important to ascertain why the dog is acting in this manner. Aggression is a display of dominance, and the dog should not have the dominant role in its pack, which is, in this case, your family.

It is important not to challenge an aggressive dog, as this could provoke an attack. Observe your Schnauzer's body language. Does he make direct eye contact and stare? Does he try to make himself as large as possible: ears pricked,

Dogs thrive on being a part of the pack, which is why separation anxiety can be a big problem in dogs of any breed.

FEAR IN A GROWN DOG

Fear in a grown dog is often the result of improper or incomplete socialisation as a pup, or it can be the result of a traumatic experience he suffered when young. Keep in mind that the term 'traumatic' is relative—something that you would not think twice about can leave a lasting negative impression on a puppy. If the dog experiences a similar experience later in life, he may try to fight back to protect himself. Again, this behaviour is very unpredictable, especially if you do not know what is triggering his fear.

chest out, tail erect? Height and size signify authority in a dog pack—being taller or 'above' another dog literally means that he is 'above' in social status. These body signals tell you that your Schnauzer thinks he is in charge—a problem that needs to be addressed. An aggressive dog is unpredictable; you never know when he is going to strike and what he is going to do. You cannot understand why a dog that is playful one minute is growling the next.

Fear is a common cause of aggression in dogs. Perhaps your Schnauzer had a negative experience as a puppy, which causes him to be fearful when a similar situation presents itself later in life. The dog may act aggressively in order to protect himself from whatever is making him afraid. It is not always easy to determine what is making your dog fearful, but if you can isolate what brings out the fear reaction, you can help the dog get over it.

Supervise your Schnauzer's interactions with people and other dogs, and praise the dog when it goes well. If he starts to act aggressively in a situation, correct him and remove him from the situation. Do not let people approach the dog and start petting him without your express permission. That way, you can command the dog to sit to accept petting, and praise him when he behaves properly. You are focusing on praise and on modifying his behaviour by rewarding him when he acts appropriately. By being gentle and by supervising his interactions, you are showing him that there is no need to be afraid or defensive.

The best solution is to consult a behavioural specialist, one who has experience with the Schnauzer if possible. Together, perhaps you can pinpoint the cause of your dog's aggression and do something about it. An aggressive dog cannot be trusted, and a dog that cannot be trusted is not safe to have as a family pet. If, very unusually, you find that your pet has become untrustworthy and you feel it necessary to seek a new home with a more suitable family and environment, explain fully to the new owners all your reasons for rehoming the dog to be fair to all concerned. In the very worst case, you will have to consider euthanasia.

AGGRESSION TOWARD OTHER DOGS
A dog's aggressive behaviour toward another dog stems from not enough exposure to other dogs

at an early age. If other dogs make your Schnauzer nervous and agitated, he will lash out as a protective mechanism. A dog that has not received sufficient exposure to other canines tends to think that he is the only dog on the planet. The animal becomes so dominant that he does not even show signs that he is fearful or threatened. Without growling or any other physical signal as a warning, he will lunge at and bite the other dog.

A way to correct this is to let your Schnauzer approach another dog when walking on lead. Watch very closely and, at the first sign of aggression, correct your Schnauzer and pull him away. Scold him for any sign of discomfort, and then praise him when he ignores the other dog. Keep this up until either he stops the aggressive behaviour, learns to ignore other dogs or even accepts other dogs. Praise him lavishly for this correct behaviour.

DOMINANT AGGRESSION
A social hierarchy is firmly established in a wild dog pack. The dog wants to dominate those under him and please those above him. Dogs know that there must be a leader. If you are not the obvious choice for emperor, the dog will assume the throne! These conflicting innate desires are what a dog owner is up against when he sets about training a dog. In

NO EYE CONTACT
If you and your on-lead dog are approached by a larger, running dog that is not restrained, walk away from the dog as quickly as possible. Do not allow your dog to make eye contact with the other dog. In dog terms, eye contact indicates a challenge. If the situation heightens, let the dogs work it out. Don't panic. Most dog fights are caused by human agitation.

DOMINANT AGGRESSION
Never allow your puppy to growl at you or bare his tiny teeth. Such behaviour is dominant and aggressive. If not corrected, the dog will repeat the behaviour, which will become more threatening as he grows larger and will eventually lead to biting.

training a dog to obey commands, the owner is reinforcing that he is the top dog in the 'pack' and that the dog should, and should want to, serve his superior. Thus, the owner is suppressing the dog's urge to dominate by modifying his behaviour and making him obedient.

An important part of training is taking every opportunity to reinforce that you are the leader. The simple action of making your Schnauzer sit to wait for his food instead of allowing him to run up to get it when he wants it says that you control when he eats; he

DOGGIE DEMOCRACY
Your dog inherited the pack-leader mentality. He only knows about pecking order. He instinctively wants to be 'top dog,' but you have to convince him that you are boss. There is no such thing as living in a democracy with your dog. You are the one who makes the rules.

is dependent on you for food. Although it may be difficult, do not give in to your dog's wishes every time he whines at you or looks at you with pleading eyes. It is a constant effort to show the dog that his place in the pack is at the bottom.

This is not meant to sound cruel or inhumane. You love your Schnauzer and you should treat him with care and affection. You (hopefully) did not get a dog just so you could control another creature. Dog training is not about being cruel or feeling important, it is about moulding the dog's behaviour into what is acceptable and teaching him to live by your rules. In theory, it is quite simple: catch him in appropriate behaviour and reward him for it. Add a dog into the equation and it becomes a bit more trying, but as a rule of thumb, positive reinforcement is what works best.

With a dominant dog, punishment and negative reinforcement can have the opposite effect of what you are after. It can make a dog fearful and/or act out aggressively if he feels he is being challenged. Remember, a dominant dog perceives himself at the top of the social heap, and will fight to defend his perceived status. The best way to prevent that is to never give him reason to think that he is in control in the first place.

If you are having trouble

Female dogs usually have two oestruses per year, with each season lasting about three weeks. These are the only times in which a female dog will mate, and she usually will not allow this until the second week of the cycle, although this varies from bitch to bitch. If not bred during the heat cycle, it is not uncommon for a bitch to experience a false pregnancy, in which her mammary glands swell and she exhibits maternal tendencies

Most dog fights are caused by human interference. Allow your Schnauzer to make the acquaintance of a friend's dog through the canine's evolved behaviour patterns. Sniffing, posturing and wrestling can be a part of the ritual.

training your Schnauzer and it seems that he is constantly challenging your authority, seek the help of an obedience trainer or behavioural specialist. A professional will work with both you and your dog to teach you effective techniques to use at home. Beware of trainers who rely on excessively harsh methods; scolding is necessary now and then, but the focus in your training should always be on positive reinforcement.

SEXUAL BEHAVIOUR

Dogs exhibit certain sexual behaviours that may have influenced your choice of male or female when you first purchased your Schnauzer. To a certain extent, spaying/neutering will eliminate these behaviours, but if you are purchasing a dog that you wish to breed from, you should be aware of what you will have to deal with throughout the dog's life.

BELLY UP!
When two dogs are introduced, they will naturally establish who is dominant. This may involve one dog placing his front paws on the other's shoulders, or one dog rolling over and exposing his belly, thereby assuming a submissive status. If neither dog submits, they may fight until one has been pinned down. This behaviour can be upsetting for owners to watch, especially if your dog takes one look and throws himself on the ground. The biggest mistake you can make is to interfere, pulling on the leads and confusing the dogs. If you don't allow them to establish their pecking order, you undermine the pack mentality, which can cause your dog great stress. If you separate dogs in the middle of a fight, the interference may incite them to attack each other viciously. Your best choice is to stay out of it!

toward toys or other objects.

With male dogs, owners must be aware that whole dogs (dogs who are not neutered) have the natural inclination to mark their territory. Males mark their territory by spraying small amounts of urine as they lift their legs in a macho ritual. Marking can occur both outdoors in the garden and around the neighbourhood as well as indoors on furniture legs, curtains and the sofa. Such behaviour can be very frustrating for the owner; early training is

DID YOU KNOW?
Dogs get to know each other by sniffing each other's backsides. It seems that each dog has a telltale odour, probably created by the anal glands. It also distinguishes sex and signals when a female will be receptive to a male's attention. Some dogs snap at another dog's intrusion of their private parts.

DID YOU KNOW?
Males, whether castrated or not, will mount almost anything: a pillow, your leg or, much to your horror, even your neighbour's leg. As with other types of inappropriate behaviour, the dog must be corrected while in the act, which for once is not difficult. Often he will not let go! While a puppy is experimenting with his very first urges, his owners feel he needs to 'sow his oats' and allow the pup to mount. As the pup grows into a full-size dog, with full-size urges, it becomes a nuisance and an embarrassment. Males always appear as if they are trying to 'save the race,' more determined and stronger than imaginable. While altering the dog at an appropriate age will limit the dog's desire, it usually does not remove it entirely.

strongly urged before the 'urge' strikes your dog. Neutering the male at an appropriate early age can solve this problem before it becomes a habit.

Other problems associated with males are wandering and mounting. Both of these habits, of course, belong to the unneutered dog, whose sexual drive leads him away from home in search of the bitch in heat. Males will mount females in heat, as well as any other dog, male or female, that happens to catch their fancy. Other possible mounting partners include his owner, the furniture, guests to the home and strangers on the street. Discourage such behaviour early on.

Owners must further recognise that mounting is not merely a sexual expression but also one of dominance exhibited in dogs and bitches alike. Be consistent and be persistent, and you will find that you can 'move mounters.'

CHEWING
The national canine pastime is chewing! Every dog loves to sink his 'canines' into a tasty bone, but sometimes that bone is in his owner's hand! Dogs need to chew, to massage their gums, to make their new teeth feel better and to exercise their jaws. This is a natural behaviour that is deeply embedded in all things canine. Our role as owners is not to stop the dog's chewing, but rather to redirect it to positive, chew-worthy objects. Be an informed owner and purchase proper chew toys, like strong

Provide your Schnauzer puppy with suitable chew toys, or he will find things of his own to massage his aching teeth and gums.

nylon bones, that will not splinter. Be sure that the objects are safe and durable, since your dog's safety is at risk. Again, the owner is responsible for ensuring a dog-proof environment.

The best answer is prevention; that is, put your shoes, handbags and other tasty objects in their proper places (out of the reach of the growing canine mouth). Direct puppies to their toys whenever you see them 'tasting' the furniture legs or the leg of your trousers. Make a loud noise to attract the pup's attention and immediately escort him to his chew toy and engage him with the toy for at least four minutes, praising and encouraging him all the while. An array of safe, interesting chew toys will keep your dog's mind and teeth occupied, and distracted from chewing on things he shouldn't.

Some trainers recommend deterrents, such as hot pepper, a bitter spice or a product designed for this purpose, to discourage the dog from chewing unwanted objects. Test these products to see which works best before investing in large quantities.

JUMPING UP
Many Schnauzers feel it is their job in the household to be the official 'jump-greet-licker' to all guests. To a dog's way of thinking, it is the best friendly way of

saying 'Hello, long-lost chum!' Some dog owners do not mind when their dog jumps up. The problem arises when guests come to the house and the dog greets them in the same manner— whether they like it or not! However friendly the greeting may be, the chances are that your visitors will not appreciate your dog's enthusiasm. The dog will not be able to distinguish upon whom he can jump and whom he cannot. Therefore, it is probably best to discourage this behaviour entirely.

Pick a command such as 'Off' (avoid using 'Down' since you will use that for the dog to lie down) and tell him 'Off' when he jumps up. Place him on the ground on all fours and have him sit, praising him the whole time. Always lavish him with praise and petting when he is in the sit position. In this way, you can give him a warm affectionate greeting, let him know that you are as excited to see him as he is to see you and instil good manners at the same time!

DIGGING

Digging, which is seen as a destructive behaviour to humans, is actually quite a natural behaviour in dogs, especially to talented earth dogs like the Schnauzers! The terriers (or 'earth dogs') are closely associated with digging, which was a large part of

NO JUMPING
Stop a dog from jumping up before he jumps. If he is getting ready to jump onto you, simply walk away. If he jumps up on you before you can turn away, lift your knee so that it bumps him in the chest. Do not be forceful. Your dog soon will realise that jumping up is not a productive way of getting attention.

their advantage in the pursuit of vermin underground.

For some dogs, digging can be irrepressible and most frustrating

Fortunately for Schnauzer owners, the breed is rather reticent in its everyday life. The Schnauzer will only interrupt his grin to bark when deemed absolutely necessary.

to their owners. When digging occurs in your garden, it is actually a normal behaviour redirected into something the dog can do in his everyday life. In the wild, a dog would be actively seeking food, making his own shelter, etc. He would be using his paws in a purposeful manner for his survival. Since you provide him with food and shelter, he has no need to use his paws for these purposes, and so the energy that he would be using may manifest itself in the form of little holes all over your garden and flower beds. If a Schnauzer is digging in your garden, he may be attempting to exterminate some wee critter that's been poking around your petunias. Naturally, the Schnauzer is not going to take kindly to being

reprimanded for doing his job.

Of course, digging is easiest to control if it is stopped as soon as possible, but it is often hard to catch a dog in the act. If your dog is a compulsive digger and is not easily distracted by other activities, you can designate an area on your property where he is allowed to dig. If you catch him digging in an off-limits area of the garden, immediately lead him to the approved area and praise him for digging there. Keep a close eye on him so that you can catch him in the act—that is the only way to make him understand what is permitted and what is not. If you take him to a crater he dug an hour ago and tell him 'No,' he will understand that you are not fond of holes, or dirt or flowers. If you catch him while he is stifle-deep in your tulips, that is when he will get your message.

SMILE!
Dogs and humans may be the only animals that smile. A dog will imitate the smile on his owner's face when he greets a friend. The dog only smiles at his human friends; he never smiles at another dog or cat. Usually, a dog rolls up his lips and shows his teeth in a clenched mouth while rolling over onto his back, begging for a soft scratch.

BARKING

Schnauzers are not extremely noisy dogs, nor are they dogs that bark just for the heck of it, although I did at one time own a Schnauzer that always gave out two distinctive 'woofs' when she first went out into the garden, and then would turn and give two more very distinctive 'woofs' just as she was about to go back into the house. I always thought of her as saying 'I'm here, world!' and 'See you later, world!'

The Schnauzer will always set off an alarm bark when he hears a strange sound. Some will bark a happy bark when they hear their owners arriving home. But woe is to the stranger that does not heed their deep warning bark.

Fortunately, Schnauzers tend to use their barks more purpose-fully than most terriers. For example, if an intruder came into your home in the middle of the night and your Schnauzer barked a warning, wouldn't you be pleased? You would probably deem your dog a hero, a wonderful guardian and protector of the home. No doubt, the Schnauzer is a formidable alarm and watchdog.

On the other hand, if a friend drops by unexpectedly, rings the doorbell and is greeted with a sudden sharp bark, you would probably be annoyed at the dog. But in reality, isn't this just the same behaviour? The dog does not know any better. Unless he sees who is at the door and it is someone he knows, he will bark as a means of vocalising that his (and your) territory is being threatened. While your friend is not posing a threat, it is all the same to the dog. Barking is his means of letting you know that there is an intrusion, whether friend or foe, on your property. The Schnauzer is an excellent and discerning family watchdog. But occasionally, if not instructed otherwise, the Schnauzer can get carried away with itself when guests arrive. I have found that a quiet 'thank you' (for the watchdog work) and saying 'that's enough now,' meaning 'quiet so I can greet my guests,' works very well. I am a firm believer in praising dogs for a job well done.

Excessive habitual barking, however, is a problem that should be corrected early on. As your Schnauzer grows up, you will be able to tell when his barking is purposeful and when it is for no reason. You will become able to distinguish your dog's different barks and their meanings. For example, the bark when someone comes to the door will be different from the bark when he is excited to see you. It is similar to a person's tone of voice, except that the dog has to rely totally on tone of voice because he does not have the benefit of using words. An incessant barker will be evident at an early age.

There are some things that encourage a dog to bark. For example, if your dog barks non-stop for a few minutes and you give him a treat to quieten him, he believes that you are rewarding him for barking. He will associate barking with getting a treat, and will keep doing it until he is rewarded. On the other hand, if you give him a command such as 'Quiet' and praise him after he has stopped barking for a few seconds, he will get the idea that being 'quiet' is what you want him to do.

FOOD STEALING

Is your dog devising ways of stealing food from your coffee table or kitchen counter? If so, you must answer the following questions: Is your Schnauzer hungry, or is he 'constantly famished' like many dogs seem to be? Face it, some dogs are more food-motivated than others. They are totally obsessed by the smell of food and can only think of their next meal. Food stealing is terrific fun and always yields a great reward—FOOD, glorious food.

Your goal as an owner, therefore, is to be sensible about where food is placed in the home and to reprimand your dog whenever he is caught in the act of stealing. But remember, only reprimand your dog if you actually see him stealing, not later when the crime is discovered; that will be of no use at all and will only serve to confuse him.

BEGGING

Just like food stealing, begging is a favourite pastime of hungry puppies! It achieves that same lovely result—FOOD! Dogs quickly learn that their owners keep the 'good food' for themselves, and that we humans do not dine on dried food alone. Begging is a conditioned response related to a specific stimulus, time and place. The sounds of the kitchen, cans and bottles opening, crinkling bags, the smell of food in preparation, etc., will excite the dog, and soon the paws will be in the air!

Here is the solution to stopping this behaviour: Never give in to a beggar! You are rewarding the dog for sitting pretty, jumping up, whining and rubbing his nose into you by giving him food. By ignoring the dog, you will (eventually) force the behaviour into extinction. Note that the behaviour is likely to get worse before it disappears, so be sure there are not any 'softies' in the family who will give in to little 'Oliver' every time he whimpers, 'More, please.'

COPROPHAGIA

Faeces eating is, to humans, one of the most disgusting behaviours that their dogs could engage in, yet, to dogs, it is perfectly normal. It is hard for us to understand why a dog would want to eat his own faeces. He could be seeking certain nutrients that are missing from his diet, he could be just plain hungry or he could be attracted by the pleasing (to a dog) scent. While coprophagia most often refers to the dog's eating his own faeces, a dog may just as likely eat that of another animal as well if he comes across it. Vets have found that diets with low levels of digestibility, containing relatively low levels of fibre and high levels of starch, increase coprophagia. Therefore, high-fibre diets may decrease the likelihood of dogs' eating faeces. Both the consistency of the stool (how firm it feels in the dog's mouth) and the presence of undigested nutrients increase the likelihood. Dogs often find the stool of cats and horses more palatable than that of other dogs. Once the dog develops diarrhoea from faeces eating, he will likely stop this distasteful habit.

To discourage this behaviour, first make sure that the food you are feeding your dog is nutritionally complete and that he is getting enough food. If changes in his diet do not seem to work, and no medical cause can be found, you will have to modify the behaviour through environmental

control before it becomes a habit. The best way to prevent your dog from eating his stool is to make it unavailable—clean up after he eliminates and remove any stool from the garden. If it is not there, he cannot eat it.

Reprimanding for stool eating rarely impresses the dog. Vets recommend distracting the dog while he is in the act of stool eating. Coprophagia is seen most frequently in pups 6 to 12 months of age, and usually disappears around the dog's first birthday.

Some Schnauzers will go to any lengths to steal victuals from your counter-tops. It's best to keep food out of the reach of your seemingly famished dog!

INDEX

My Schnauzer

PUT YOUR PUPPY'S FIRST PICTURE HERE

Dog's Name _____

Date _____ Photographer _____